P9-CPW-624

The Art *of* Mindful Reading

The Art of Mindful Reading

Embracing the Wisdom of Words

Ella Berthoud

Leaping Hare Press

First published in the UK and North America in 2019 by

Leaping Hare Press

An imprint of The Quarto Group
The Old Brewery, 6 Blundell Street, London N7 9BH, United Kingdom
T (0)20 7700 6700 **F** (0)20 7700 8066
www.QuartoKnows.com

Text © 2019 Ella Berthoud
Design and layout © 2019 Quarto Publishing plc

All rights reserved. No part of this book may be reproduced
or transmitted in any form or by any means, electronic or mechanical, including
photocopying, recording, or by any information storage and retrieval system,
without written permission from the copyright holder.

British Library Cataloguing-in-Publication Data
A catalogue record for this book is available from the British Library

ISBN: 978-1-78240-768-3

This book was conceived, designed and produced by

Leaping Hare Press

58 West Street, Brighton BN1 2RA, United Kingdom
Publisher SUSAN KELLY
Creative Director MICHAEL WHITEHEAD
Editorial Director TOM KITCH
Commissioning Editor MONICA PERDONI
Project Editor CAROLINE EARLE
Design Manager ANNA STEVENS
Designer GINNY ZEAL
Illustrator MELVYN EVANS

Printed in China

1 3 5 7 9 10 8 6 4 2

Contents

INTRODUCTION

*Reading — it's one of the first things we do
in life, sitting on our loved ones' laps and enjoying
the soothing voice of a parent explaining the world
through pictures and words. Collections of letters on
the page become sounds, images and thoughts that
activate our imagination, language and ability to
communicate. What begins as a jumble of marks, black
against white, conjures colours, monsters and beasts,
emotions, laughter and tears. Eventually, the process
of changing squiggles into words becomes as natural to
us as breathing — and just as necessary. Read on to
discover how mind and spirit become one through
diving into the art of reading mindfully.*

A Love Of Reading

◆

Reading is a pastime embraced by almost every culture in the modern world. Young and old, male and female, everyone reads (unless they have been raised by wolves) and reading is an inescapable part of life. For some, it is simply a functional habit, like eating to stay alive. For others, like me, it's something we crave like a cactus craves sunshine. Without it, we would crinkle up.

WHEN I WAS FIVE YEARS OLD, my parents took me and my brother on a journey from Iran to Finland, driving in a Wolseley 1300. In those days we had no seatbelts, and I lay on the parcel shelf, with a stack of picture books. I decided I was going to learn to read, and I copied out the letters on each page, proudly showing them to my parents at the end of each day. I got through *Ferdinand* as we drove through Turkey, *The Cat in the Hat* as we traversed Hungary and *Struwwelpeter* as we sped around Germany. My brother Chris could already read, and he helped me to master the alphabet. By the time we reached Helsinki, I was firmly addicted to the magic of the page. Nothing could tear me away from a book, be it the cotton fields of Isfahan, or the metre-thick ice of Helsinki harbour. At first, delighted that I had been kept so well distracted during this three-week journey, undeterred through an avalanche and a heatwave, my parents soon began to wonder – was I going to miss out on life through reading too much?

My mother was my first role model for reading – it was her default entertainment, and she would never be without a book. Omnivorous in her literary consumption, she would read everything from sci-fi and crime to literary fiction, memoir, science books and magazines.

I was one of four children – myself and three brothers – and many was the moment when we would play 'Cowboys and Indians' with guns, bows and arrows, a shouting, whirling mass of noise and bodies in mayhem around her, while she sat oblivious to it all, reading a book. She was able to switch off from everything around her and read with absolute concentration. This ability to disappear into a book was the first time I saw mindful reading in action. My mother put all her being into the book at that moment in time, and made the absolute most of her reading time. I learnt to copy her, and was soon lost in my own books, in parallel with my omnivorous parent. In our noisy household, I could be lost for hours on end, curled up in a chair, my body present but my head somewhere far away – Narnia, with the four siblings who become kings, or the jungles of Africa with Tarzan, or joining in with the adventures of Tintin.

Understanding the World Through Reading

As a bibliotherapist, I embrace and rely on reading; it's as important to me as food. My job involves looking at the entire person – their life, their tastes, their passions, desires, hopes, dreams and any issues they may have. I then prescribe the ideal books for them to read right now – according to what is happening in their lives at the moment, what new paths they might be taking or what major life events are happening to them. I aim to give the right books to the right people at the right time in their lives, and therefore I take reading as a pastime very seriously.

Children learn empathy, moral codes and social norms through the stories they are read as tots, then when they are old enough, the stories they read to themselves, and then the books they read as teens. Our understanding of the world is shaped throughout our lives by reading – newspapers, novels, biographies, non-fiction and online. As a bibliotherapist, I believe that every novel you read shapes the person that you are, speaking to you on a deep, unconscious level, and altering your very nature with the ideas that it shows you. With every novel you absorb, you live a life that is different to your own, and this affects you on a fundamental level. Reading mindfully, as I will show, can help you to reflect meaningfully on the texts that you read, whether they are fiction, newspapers, online journalism, poems or non-fiction.

> *With every novel you absorb, you live a life that is different to your own, and this affects you on a fundamental level.*

The benefits of reading can be seen not just in terms of what you learn, but also of their impact on your mental health – even your physical health is affected by reading. A recent study has shown that readers of fiction live on average two years longer than non-readers. Yes! It's true. Reading makes you live longer. When you read, your heart rate slows, your eyes 'saccade' across the page, back and forth, which is a movement that creates a stress-reducing meditative state in your brain. Studies have shown that when the brain is in a reading state, it is very similar to the state that the brain attains when practising meditation. You could say that reading effectively *is* mindfulness personified. I have developed various exercises that will help you to make your reading more mindful, which will be shown throughout this book.

If reading is your daily bread, then how best should it be consumed? And how should you read mindfully? Why will reading mindfully help you read better? That's what I'm going to explore in this book.

CHAPTER ONE

LOSE YOURSELF
IN A BOOK

*In this chapter, I will discuss the joy of reading, and
how to return to that feeling of forgetting yourself in
a book. Together we investigate why reading is
emotionally good for you, and how you might
mindfully use reading to develop your
emotional intelligence.*

WHAT KIND OF READER ARE YOU?

◆

Do you read aloud in your head? Do you see images in your brain while you read? Are you hearing the words, or speaking them silently — or even audibly? Might you have an urge to act out, in your mind, the events in the book?

THINK ABOUT WHAT HAPPENS when you read a book. Do you hear each word in your head as you read it? Do you internally use accents for the characters in the novel? Is every word pronounced in your head, or do you flow them together and only hear some of them? Do you move your lips while you read, in sync with the words in your brain? Or is your reading more of a visual feast — you vividly picture the scene described, visualizing every leaf, snowflake or blade of grass. Do you see the scene in colour, or in black and white? Is your vision based on images you have seen before that are connected with this book (such as from the cover, artwork or a movie version of the book), or are they invented for you now? Finally, are you someone who wants to be literally in the scene? When you read about pouring a cup of tea, do you find your hand involuntarily moving? Are your feet kicking if you read about someone running or playing football? Or do you have something to fiddle with while you are reading, like a stress ball?

If you are the first kind of reader, who internally voices every word, you are more of an audio type of reader. This means that it could suit you very well to listen to audiobooks more and embrace them into your life. You might be a little bit slower as a reader, but you may find that you remember books better. If you do listen to audiobooks, you will remember the voice of the narrator, and the book will forever be associated with that voice. If you still tend to read rather than listen, your own inner voice will be the one that you remember.

Do you hear each word in your head as you read it? Do you use accents for the characters? Or is your reading more of a visual feast?

If you are the second type of reader, you will think of everything to do with the book in terms of images. The entire book will be shown to you in technicolour, and you might remember it more like a film. This means that you have a strong visual imagination, and are likely to remember the visual aspects of the book you are reading — landscape, colours, physical descriptions of people and so on.

If you are the third kind of reader, you are kinaesthetic. You want to interact physically with what you are reading — you may want to highlight passages in different colours, doodle in the margin or get up and walk around while reading. If music is playing while you read, this will help you to remember it, and if smells are wafting in your vicinity, these will be integrated into your reading experience.

MINDFULNESS EXERCISE

DISCOVER A NEW AWARENESS OF READING

✳

Read this passage mindfully, carefully considering what kind of a reader you might be.

There was a table set out under a tree in front of the house, and the March Hare and the Hatter were having tea at it: a Dormouse was sitting between them, fast asleep, and the other two were using it as a cushion, resting their elbows on it, and then talking over its head. 'Very uncomfortable for the Dormouse,' thought Alice, 'only, as it's asleep, I suppose it doesn't mind.'

The table was a large one, but the three were all crowded together at one corner of it: `No room! No room!' they cried out when they saw Alice coming. 'There's PLENTY of room!' said Alice indignantly, and she sat down in a large arm-chair at one end of the table.

'Have some wine,' the March Hare said in an encouraging tone.

Alice looked all round the table, but there was nothing on it but tea. 'I don't see any wine,' she remarked.

'There isn't any,' said the March Hare.

'Then it wasn't very civil of you to offer it,' said Alice angrily.

'It wasn't very civil of you to sit down without being invited,' said the March Hare.

'I didn't know it was YOUR table,' said Alice, 'it's laid for a great many more than three.'

'Your hair wants cutting,' said the Hatter. He had been looking at Alice for some time with great curiosity, and this was his first speech.

'You should learn not to make personal remarks,' Alice said with some severity, 'it's very rude.'

The Hatter opened his eyes very wide on hearing this; but all he SAID was, 'Why is a raven like a writing-desk?'

'Come, we shall have some fun now!' thought Alice. 'I'm glad they've begun asking riddles — I believe I can guess that,' she added aloud.

'Do you mean that you think you can find out the answer to it?' said the March Hare.

'Exactly so,' said Alice.

'Then you should say what you mean,' the March Hare went on.

'I do,' Alice hastily replied; `at least – at least I mean what I say – that's the same thing, you know.'

'Not the same thing a bit!' said the Hatter. `You might just as well say that "I see what I eat" is the same thing as "I eat what I see"!'

'You might just as well say,' added the March Hare, 'that "I like what I get" is the same thing as "I get what I like"!'

'You might just as well say,' added the Dormouse, who seemed to be talking in his sleep, 'that "I breathe when I sleep" is the same thing as "I sleep when I breathe"!'

'It IS the same thing with you,' said the Hatter, and here the conversation dropped, and the party sat silent for a minute, while Alice thought over all she could remember about ravens and writing-desks, which wasn't much.

From Alice in Wonderland by Lewis Carroll

Do you internally use different accents for the Mad Hatter, for Alice and the dormouse? Do you vividly picture the long table with its motley crew at one end – Hatter, Dormouse, March Hare and, of course Alice – all sitting round a collection of tea things.? Do you see the scene in colour, or in black and white? Is your vision based on the illustrations you have observed in your own *Alice in Wonderland* book, or are they invented for you now? When you read about pouring a cup of tea, do you find your hand involuntarily moving? Are your feet kicking like Alice's might be, while you look around for evidence of wine? Do you feel an urge to reach across the Dormouse while he sleeps?

RECOGNIZE THE KIND OF READER YOU ARE

◆

Recognizing what kind of a reader you are will help you to deepen your reading experience. It is illuminating to examine your reading process, and think about the way your brain experiences the transference of meaning from the series of letters written on the page into words that awaken your senses visually, orally and kinaesthetically.

Are You an Auditory Reader?

If you are an auditory type of reader, you would benefit hugely from spending more time reading aloud, or being read to. Try reading aloud with your partner, your children or your friends, or in a group. Sit by a fire of a wintery night and share a story with some good dialogue, and opportunities for using your voice in different ways. A ghost story could be read aloud in a quiet, querulous voice, crescendoing into dramatic shouts, sinking down into whispers; you can add your own sound effects with knocks on the door, creepy scratches under your listener's seat, or by running your nail along a piece of wood. You can practise your accents, opening up a world of exciting voices, and also vary the pace of your reading – deliberately speeding up and slowing down for dramatic effect. Soon you will relish the auditory potential of the words on the page, and be fully aware of their rhythm, their internal rhymes and their punctuation, enjoying more and more the ways you can use these to your benefit as a reader.

Are You a Visual Reader?

If you are a visual kind of reader, you should choose books with a strong visual theme so as to enter most fully into the fictional world. Books like *Tess of the D'Urbervilles*, and indeed all of Hardy's writing, are rich with visual depictions that take you to the places described so vividly that you feel like you live in the cottage with the farm gable, or the hut on the edge of a stormy field. When you read your next book, immerse yourself fully in its visual world. Ponder every image for longer than you normally would. If the writer describes the snow that has crept in through a chink in the door, relish that image for a couple of minutes. Picture exactly what it would look like, adding in the missing elements – how big is the cone of powdery snow, what would the footprints look like on the floor and what exactly would a snow-mist look, feel and taste like? Extend your visual insights into your other senses, and allow yourself to enter the scene even more fully.

Are you a Kinaesthetic Reader?

If you are a kinaesthetic kind of reader, there are a few ways that you can enter into your reading more intensely. Walk around while reading the book. (This may seem odd at first, but try it. It is something you can do! Just look up every now and then so you don't crash into a table or tree). Go and read in an unusual place – in a park, in your garden, on a swing-seat where you can rock yourself gently as you read.

Play music while you read – gentle music in the background will help you to remember what you have read, and still your mind and body so that you can more easily lose yourself in the book. Some people prefer silence, however; it depends what works best for you.

Doodle in the pages, highlight phrases, turn down the corners of pages – interact physically with the book. Don't worry about the book being a sacrosanct object. It's yours! (If you got it from the library, be more circumspect though – perhaps just leave a message in gentle pencil for the next reader.) Gone are the days when a book cost you more than a month's wages. In my view, books are improved by the marks we leave on them – especially if it's a mark that is a reaction to something you have read. When you re-read the book, that coffee stain, footprint or splodge of mayonnaise from your sandwich will bring back happy memories of what you were doing when you first read the book. If you are a kinaesthetic reader, the body memories left by triggering marks like these will help you to remember the book. If you doodle on the page while reading, and the doodle relates in any way either to the thoughts you are having about the book or to the place you are in when you are reading it, this will help you to remember more about the reading experience, not just what you were reading, but where you were when you were reading – what you felt, touched, smelt and even thought during that particular reading moment.

ACTING OUT SCENES FROM A BOOK

✳

Sometimes it can be illuminating to act out scenes from a book. In the passage below, Tess is about to perform hard manual labour in the snow. Inspired by this scene, you could wrap up warm and head outside to do something that seems pointless (polish the stones on your drive, cut your grass with scissors). Gradually the 'pointlessness' will transmute into mindfulness.

Then one day a peculiar quality invaded the air of this open country. There came a moisture which was not of rain, and a cold which was not of frost. It chilled the eyeballs of the twain, made their brows ache, penetrated to their skeletons, affecting the surface of the body less than its core. They knew that it meant snow, and in the night the snow came. Tess, who continued to live at the cottage with the warm gable that cheered any lonely pedestrian who paused beside it, awoke in the night, and heard above that thatch noises which seemed to signify that the roof had turned itself into a gymnasium of all the winds. When she lit her lamp to get up in the morning she found that the snow had blown through a chink in the casement, forming a white cone of the finest powder against the inside, and had also come down the chimney, so that it lay sole-deep upon the floor, on which her shoes left tracks when she moved about. Without, the storm drove so fast as to create a snow-mist in the kitchen; but as yet it was too dark out-of-doors to see anything.

The snow had followed the birds from the polar basin as a white pillar of a cloud, and individual flakes could not be seen. The blast smelt of icebergs, arctic seas, whales, and white bears, carrying the snow so that it licked the land but did not deepen on it. They trudged onwards with slanted bodies through the flossy fields, keeping as well as they could in the shelter of hedges, which, however, acted as strainers rather than screens.

From *Tess of the D'Urbervilles* by Thomas Hardy

Deep Reading

Having established what kind of a reader you are, now spend some time 'deep reading' the passage on page 21. If you are a visual reader, you will picture that 'cone of snow' with great clarity. Do you see it as a solid cone, like sugar, or is it hazy, like talcum powder? Do you see Tess's footprints in the whiteness, and if so, what are they like? The 'disordered medley of greys' will swirl around your head and give you an impression of dawn mist emerging from the night. The 'achromatic chaos of things' will rob your brain of colour and send you into a half-sleep, lulling you into a dream state.

When you look more closely at each passage, you can sink more deeply into the words.

If your brain is more of an audio-type reading muscle, you will focus on the sounds of the words themselves. *Snow*, *blown* and *cone* will all play musically in your mind, creating assonance with the 'o' sound, which Hardy has focused on to add to the atmosphere of woe. In the next paragraph, Hardy uses staccato sounds to evoke the whistling of the snow through the hedges. When you look more closely at each passage, you can sink more deeply into the words and the ideas and images they evoke, so that you are more and more lost in the author's vision. You can apply this mindful technique to all kinds of reading – it will be particularly powerful in poetry, literary fiction and all artistic forms of writing.

Reading Poetry Mindfully

◆

Poetry is a great area of literature to practise your mindfulness techniques on. Poems are, in a way, mindful meditations on an idea or a creature, a metaphor or a paradox. They offer us a window into a new way of looking at something of the everyday.

F IND SOME OF YOUR FAVOURITE POEMS – they could be verses that you read as a child or ones that you have discovered in more recent years. Look very closely at the text. Read it aloud. Allow the words to trip off your palate. Listen to the sussurations of your tongue, make yourself aware of the breaths you take when reading the poems aloud. Listen to repeated sounds, to consonants, vowels and rhymes and half-rhymes. Say the poem to yourself several times – both aloud and internally. The more you say it, the more you will begin to understand it and to grapple with its meaning. Those words that you first noticed and which might have seemed obscure and opaque will begin to make a different kind of sense. By repeating the poem to yourself many times, or reading it aloud to a friend, the meaning will begin to be divulged. Look for the intention behind the words. Is that surface interpretation actually what the poem is about? Is it a metaphor, with a hidden meaning? Could it be describing not just the idea on the surface, but also something deeper and more universal?

Now read the poem one last time, and simply let the words flow into your brain. Resist actively thinking about what it all means and just enjoy reading it. The meaning will have changed as you have thought about the poem so much, and now you will have a full and rich understanding of it.

Learn the Poem by Heart

Finally, as your last mindful exercise with this poem, learn it off by heart. Say the words to yourself over and over again until they stick in your head. You will find this process nourishing, like repeating a mantra, and each time you say the poem to yourself, new meanings and thoughts will occur to you. Sometimes you will just seem to hear the sounds of the poem, and not necessarily think too deeply about what they mean. At other times you will think hard about every word, sound and image. You will become more aware of assonance – when vowels in nearby words rhyme with each other – and dissonance – a harsh collection of sounds – and also of rhythm, rhyme and structure.

The point of doing this, and of learning any poem, is to be able to call on a poem at any time as a means of soothing your thoughts and calming a swirling brain. Anyone who has a collection of poems within their mind that they can summon at will, will find that in times of boredom, stress or even crisis, a poem will help them to calm down, breathe, slow their heartbeat, and be comforted and soothed.

CREATING A READING NOOK

◆

What reader does not crave a reading nook, a space just for them, where they can curl up with a good book, for hours on end, uninterrupted by phone, man or beast? Every reader should have their own nook, and it is far easier to create than you might imagine.

IMAGINE A PLACE WHERE YOU CAN RETREAT from the world with a good book. A place where no one else can find you (unless you want to be found), where you feel safe and where you can lose yourself in a book. Now, having imagined it, you need to create it. Before you start, think about where is the best place to escape into your reading world most mindfully. You will need a place that's quiet, calm and uncluttered. If you live in a house with lots of other people – children, dogs, housemates – try to make your nook in a place where they won't disturb you. Consider putting a curtain in front of it, or even a screen, so that you can stay behind it for those vital minutes or hours of reading replenishment. A canopy can also be created, using a hoop and some light fabric, cocooning you in your world of words. Make your nook anywhere in your house – halfway up the stairs on a landing, an improvised day-bed in a study, in a hanging chair near a fire or simply in the corner of a room, where you can put cosy cushions, a book-shelf, a platform for a cup of tea, and a nice rug to sit or lie on. Spend some time making your reading nook irresistible.

Would you prefer a beanbag, a pile of cushions or a favourite chair to sit on? Perhaps you can make a bespoke seating arrangement within an alcove or a bay window, like Jane Eyre's reading spot behind the curtains in the Reeds' living-room, a sanctuary from the household around her.

Make it cosy, a place where you can curl up comfortably, with everything you need to hand. You might want a place to put a drink and a couple of biscuits. A small shelf that's easy to reach would be perfect for this. You will also need a bookshelf for your favourite books. You will, of course, keep your current reading book there (unless you have it about your person at all times, as many of us do). You can also keep a few favourite books there, the ones you always return to, which you know you can rely on and you might want to dip into randomly. Keep a comfort book there too – one you've read many times, that's dog-eared and loved, and which perhaps you have had for years. That way, when you just have a few minutes to relax in your reading nook, you can plonk yourself down with no preparation at all – when you are passing by, heave a sigh of relief and settle into your nook.

Now you have begun to think about different ways of getting lost in a book, and of how you can be mindful while you read. You have taken some time to think about what kind of a reader you are, and how you can get more out of your reading. In the next chapter, you can begin to think about different approaches to the act of reading.

Outdoor Nooks

If your reading nook is outside, make it as comfortable as possible. If you are lucky enough to have a treehouse, it could be in there. In a warm climate, fill the nook with cushions, perhaps a soft blanket to put around you if a chill develops, and again, you must have that vital shelf for a cocktail, juice or glass of wine. This shelf could be a natural one, formed by branches, or a shelf in a grassy bank, or you could construct it from natural materials. For the reading spot itself, you could use a hammock, or create a reading 'orb' using willow or carefully steamed hardwood. Tents are also a possibility, as are swinging chairs or you can make a temporary reading spot with just a rug, cushions and a canopy for shade. Encourage your family to make their own reading nooks outside, and on Sundays, spend an hour or two out there with them, all absorbed in your own books, or reading aloud from one book together. This will hopefully become a habit, and everyone will love their outside reading time. In rainy weather, you might have a reading bower or a hut at the end of the garden, where you can all hole up with a book. People living in extreme climates could get even more inventive, with a reading igloo, or a reading oasis with hammock … the possibilities are endless.

CHAPTER TWO

WAYS OF READING

*How do we find different practical approaches to
reading that can also be mindful? People seek all kinds
of things in what they read — knowledge, wisdom,
emotional intelligence, excitement, escapism and
catharsis. At different times of our lives, we want
different things from reading. The way we read matters
too. In this chapter, I will help you to think about
different ways of reading. You can break the habitual
patterns of your mind by reading, effectively
rearranging the circuits of your brain.*

THE HEALING POWER OF READING

Since the time of Plato, people have been aware of the beneficial powers of reading, and of vicariously experiencing strong emotions through the power of fiction, whether this is by reading, or by watching a play. Plato said 'books give a soul to the universe, wings to the mind, flight to the imagination and life to everything.'

THE GREEKS HAD THE WISDOM to build theatres next to hospitals, so that their patients could be healed not just by medicine, but also by art. One aspect of this that they were particularly aware of was catharsis, which can be described as a technique of purging powerfully felt emotions, particularly through artistic expression. The release of strong emotions was seen as healing, and that holds true to this day.

Lose Yourself

When we read a good novel, we lose ourselves in its pages in a way that is unique to this art form. Because we spend a certain amount of time living with these characters, absorbing their thoughts and feelings, effectively living their lives through the pages of the book, we invest more of our true selves in the characters than we would while watching a film or a drama on TV. By the time we have finished the book, we have entered wholeheartedly in their lives, and we have in a way *become* those characters, taking on their thoughts and feelings. If they have gone through great events, we have been on an emotional seesaw with them. We have let out our own emotions through the medium of their loves and losses. In the novel *Me Before You* by Jojo Moyes, a girl named Louisa looks after Will Traynor, a formerly vastly successful businessman who has had an accident and lost all movement from the neck down. Reading their story, we fall in love with Will along with Louisa, and agonize with her over her desire to help him to live life to the full – even though he wants to end it all. Most people reading this book are soon openly weeping in public. And then they say how much they loved the book.

Catharsis

Why do we have this huge desire to experience tragedy in fiction? This because we need *catharsis*, the experience of suffering vicariously through various art forms, which results in purification or purgation. Through reading of Will and Louisa's tragic love, we purge ourselves of our own emotions, and ultimately feel cleansed and renewed. We are invigorated by tragedy in art, feeling more alive as a result of experiencing it. By reading about a tragic love story, we can purge our own feelings and feel happy that we have a comparatively good and uncomplicated life. Our own worries fly out the window as we lose ourselves in fiction. It would be boring if the fictional characters we read about were all happy, and nothing went wrong in their lives.

Reading and the Brain

Learning to read is not actually an easy process. It takes our brains years to make the connections and circuits that lead us to turn the black and white characters on the page first into meaningful letters, then into words, and finally into words that we read without thinking. We have to see a written word more than two hundred times before it becomes intuitively understandable to our brain. Repetition is key to learning to read, which is why the more we read, the quicker we can do it.

Some people have problems with reading that are caused by the way that their brains are wired. Dyslexia, hyperlexia and attention deficit hyperactivity disorder (ADHD) all affect reading in different ways, and can be helped with various approaches, which I will touch upon later in this chapter.

Neuroscientists have shown that the reading brain is calmed and slowed while reading, in a way that is very similar to the effects of meditation. Reading can therefore be shown to be effective in combating stress and anxiety.

Reading in Daily Life

◆

The reading exercise on pages 34–35 is based on our most instinctive, thoughtless process of reading, which is here turned into an exercise in mindfulness. Words that normally are read almost without any awareness, are examined and cogitated thoroughly. But now let's turn to the kind of reading that we are all conscious of doing in our daily lives — the reading of books for pleasure, for self-education or for work.

Many of us love to read fiction, but find it difficult to put the time into this valuable and relaxing activity. As a bibliotherapist, I often find that people imagine reading fiction is a self-indulgent thing to do, and that they ought to be doing something else. Much research has been conducted into the benefits of reading fiction, which deepens your empathy and emotional intelligence, helps with making important life decisions and allows your brain to rest. Research has shown that reading provides as much relaxation as meditation, and just six minutes reading can de-stress more than listening to music, drinking tea or going for a walk. If you become absorbed in a gripping story, you actually enter an altered state of consciousness. You are literally *lost* in a book, experiencing a temporary absence from the real world – your heart rate slows, your muscles unwind, worries are forgotten and you are in another state both mentally and physically.

MINDFULNESS EXERCISE

BE AWARE OF EVERYTHING YOU READ

❋

Reading is something that we do without noticing all the time, on our phones, on street signs and advertising hoardings, newsstands and magazines. Even the briefest of readings can be turned into a mindful exercise.

Next time you walk down a street, notice all the different moments when you read a word or collection of words. A walk from home to work will almost inevitably provide many reading moments. A shop sign, a bus timetable, posters at a train station, a glimpse into a newsagent with news headlines and magazine articles.

Make a mental note of each different type of written word you encounter on your walk:

- How big is the writing?
- What is the font like?
- How does the word make you feel?
- If it is big, golden and curvy, perhaps on a sign for a bakery, does it seem friendly and positive?
- If it is a news headline consisting of a few snappy words, is it perhaps rather grim and depressing?
- Think for a minute about how that word was actually created. Did someone stand up on a ladder and paint it onto a shop wall? Or did a sign maker create it somewhere else, using a computer, then put it in situ?
- Was a newspaper headline printed in a local depot, then slapped up outside this newsagent in the early hours of the morning?
- Perhaps you glimpse words on a board inside a café, listing what's on the menu this morning. A waitress may have carefully used their best cursive script to write these words using chalk, or a chalk pen, perhaps having to re-write sections to make them fit beautifully onto the space available.

Pondering all these different ways of writing, the different approaches, methods of production and end results, is an interesting mindful exercise. It could be that you are in a foreign country, and the words and letters are alien to you. If so, dwell on the beauty of the foreign letters, seeing them purely as an abstract art form. Consider how these letters differ from our own, and whether they make any sense to you. See how shapes repeat themselves, and ponder how writing evolved into the state it now inhabits in this century. Cast your mind back to medieval times, when writing was mostly done by monks, in beautiful, huge books, ornately coloured and decorated over painstaking hours, weeks and years. Compare this labour to the instant ability we have now to make words on pages, using biros, pencils or keyboards that tap characters into existence in seconds.

Take this exercise to the next level by practising mindful writing. Before you start, place a piece of paper and a pencil near you. Now breathe in slowly and allow your mind to calm. Breathe out again and let all the stresses of the day, the distracting sounds, the niggling worries, roll away from you. Breathe in again, and this time, inhale with full awareness of your lungs filling up with air. Then release the air, and with it, release any preconceptions about how writing works. Pick up your pencil and write your own name. Write it first without thinking about the lettering. Then write it again, big and bold. Write it small and with very little pressure. Look at all these different ways of writing, and think for a moment about the incredible way that each letter represents a sound. As proficient readers, these letters are hotwired into our brains and we are unconscious of them as individual letters, reading them as whole words instead. Meditate on the way that writing has evolved over the millennia, from scratches on wood and stone, to chalk on slate, to writing in wax, to pen and ink, to print on paper, and to pixels on a screen. Where would we be without writing? It is as essential to our species as clothing.

Seize the Mindful Moment

According to Dr David Lewis of Mindlab International, you should always be prepared to snatch a reading opportunity, even if you are just grabbing six minutes at a time. Have a book either to hand in physical form, or downloaded onto an e-reader or your phone. Screens are generally less relaxing on the eyes than paper books, but if you can't have a book in your bag, a screen is definitely sensible. Then, when you are on your way to or from work, even in a crowded tube, train or bus, there are few of us who won't have six minutes to grab. Make it a mission to read in your lunch break if you can too. So many of us don't factor in a lunch break, instead finding a sandwich and eating it at the desk, or snatching a coffee and not sitting down for a break. Schedule in a mindful period of your day when you sit down somewhere with a book and a sandwich, and read. Reading a few pages while you eat, sitting on a park bench, or in a café, in a quiet room in your office or under a tree, can create a time of escape from the tribulations of work and your busy day, on that will make a huge difference to your wellbeing. Take the radical step of turning off your phone while you do this, so that nothing can disturb you.

Haiku

Some people prefer to meditate over poetry rather than prose, especially if they lack time. Keep a collection of haiku to hand, whether it's a published anthology, or haiku you have found yourself and transcribed into a small notebook. Haiku is an ancient form of Japanese poetry often containing (in English) a total of seventeen syllables shared between three lines that are arranged in a pattern of 5-7-5. The first line consists of five syllables, the second line seven and the last line contains another five syllables. Original haiku poetry was measured in sounds, or 'breaths', not English syllables. The 5-7-5 approach was a rough approximation and gives a framework for English-language haiku writers, but since poetry is art, and art breaks rules, one can interpret the form in different ways. Here is a classic example of a haiku translated into English:

In the twilight rain

these brilliant-hued hibiscus . . .

A lovely sunset

'IN THE TWILIGHT RAIN'
MATSUO BASHŌ (1644–1694)

Most haiku traditionally contain a seasonal reference (here, the hibiscus, which tells us that this is the summer, when hibiscus flower), and juxtapose two ideas that might traditionally oppose each other, or reveal a new way of looking at things. In this haiku, the sunset could refer to the colours of the hibiscus or the colours in the sky. Our minds blend the two together. If you focus on the poem mindfully, you will first envisage the twilight rain. We would imagine rain falling at twilight to be soft and gentle, like twilight itself. Then we imagine the brilliant-hued hibiscus, which will be big, floppy and bright, with a long stamen. Hibiscus are quite vulnerable, delicate flowers, even though they can be large and garish. The twilight rain falling on these must create a quiet, caressing mist. Then we ponder the lovely sunset – if it is raining, the sunset must be misty but drenched with colour. Perhaps the sunset looks like hibiscus flowering in the sky – oranges, pinks and yellows reaching up, thrusting their hues into the darkness of the sky.

MINDFULNESS EXERCISE

WRITE A HAIKU

✳

Bring a notebook with you to work. In your next break, after you have read some haiku and begun to understand the process, write your own. You could describe the previous evening, or something you can see as you sit and write – a cherry tree in blossom, a bird picking up crumbs, a piece of litter scooting across the street. Try to do it once a week at first. Then, perhaps do it every day. It could be something that you do at home, to summarize your day. The act of meditating on the words, finding the right number of syllables and generating ideas from something that you see in the moment, is a wonderful way to enter a mindful state. Linking something natural to something symbolic, perhaps something in your life – a state of mind, a problem, or something to celebrate – will create poetry out of the things you observe in your everyday life.

The more you think about it, the more you can extract meaning from the poem. Allow the words to mull around your brain for as long as you can. Think about the fact that this is a translation. The translator could have written 'evening' rain instead of 'twilight'. What difference would that have made? Is twilight more romantic and evocative than evening? Twilight is the time between two worlds, between night and day, between the world of daylight and the world of night-time. It implies magic, fairies, creatures scuttling to their homes for the night, a time full of possibility and portent. Evening, on the other hand, is more prosaic – simply describing a time of day. 'Brilliant-hued' is also an interesting choice of words. Brilliant suggests bright, shiny, iridescent, almost. The translator could have used a different word to suggest brightness and intensity, but brilliant was their choice, searing something strong across the reader's inner eye. In the first poem, the contrast is between the intensity of the colours and the gentleness of the sunset. In the haiku below, the contrast is more obvious, between hot and cold.

◆

You make the fire

I'll show you something wonderful

a big ball of snow!

'A BALL OF SNOW'
MATSUO BASHŌ (1644–1694)

◆

Reading haiku takes you far away into other times in history, into other parts of the world and into states of mind that will surprise, energize and inspire you, giving you a new burst of vigour for your return to work. Now, the next thing is to try writing a haiku yourself (see page 38).

MAKE READING A DAILY HABIT

For many adults, the habit of reading is one that falls by the wayside once we start the world of work, and over recent times, people have found themselves more and more drawn to their phones or screens rather than to reading books; social media has replaced the go-to distraction of a book when standing in a queue, stuck on a journey or waiting for a friend in a café. It's all the more important therefore, to have some set times of the day when you will read. You need to discover the one that works best for you, but if you try all of these, you will find that at least one of them sticks.

Reading When You First Wake Up

For many people, this is a perfect time to read. Fresh from sleep, but not yet ready to greet the day, you roll over and pick up your book. You will quickly slip into its welcoming pages, and spend the next ten to fifteen minutes being taken to another world, before you are compelled out of bed to get on with your daily routine. A lot of readers say that this is an ideal time to escape into fiction, or pore over non-fiction, and that their brains are particularly receptive at this time of day. For the night owls, this may not be so good, but early birds will thrive at this time. It's also reliable – you tend to know where you are going to be when you wake up (unless you are backpacking around the world, sofa-surfing or in an unfortunate position of homelessness. But even then, I hope, you will always have your book in your backpack).

Reading Over Breakfast

Depending on your household situation, reading while you eat breakfast can be a perfect opportunity to relish the moment between sleep and your working day. You are up and ready for action, but perhaps not feeling completely geared to embrace the effort of thinking about practical matters. Instead, while you eat your toast or muesli, eggs or broth, place your book on a reading stand and dive back into the story. You may only have five minutes to read at this stage, but this can be a moment of particular concentration. Fresh from your night's sleep, your brain is especially receptive, and as you nourish your body with food, you can also nourish your brain with brain-food. Non-fiction can be most stimulating at this time of day – it could be a moment to read that popular science book, history or economic analysis. Save the news for your journey to work, and allow these calm minutes to be a time of absorption of information into your freshly scrubbed synapses.

Reading on the Way to Work

If you take the train to work, this can be a perfect opportunity for reading. Many people need this time to prepare for the day ahead with emails and work-related reading, but some relish the chance to remain in a bubble of fictional fun, or reading for self-betterment. If you travel on a crowded bus, tram or train, consider listening to audiobooks. Listening to audiobooks on your way to work, when you are perhaps not fully awake, can be an ideal way to experience a novel – all you need to do is sit back and listen, with the added benefit that the voice you listen to will read things more slowly than you would to yourself. Try to fit in at least ten minutes of reading on the way to work, even if you have real work to do as well. The escape into another world will refresh your brain and revitalize your neurons in a way that will ultimately benefit your working life.

Reading in Your Lunch Break

Grabbing a sandwich as you sit at your desk is an increasingly common work habit, and getting out of the office for lunch is a luxury that most of us don't give ourselves any more. But if you can escape from the hurly-burly of work for half an hour, make sure that you take your book or e-reader. Find a nice place to sit, preferably a cosy café where you won't be disturbed by your workmates, or a park bench under a beautiful cherry-blossom canopy, a secret nook in your local municipal garden or even, dare I mention it, a local library. Then, while you sip a coffee or eat your sushi, take out your book and read for ten minutes, twenty if you can fit it in.

This is an instance when I would urge you to delve into fiction rather than non-fiction. Read a short story, or a chapter of a book that you can carry on with later or the next day. It's a perfect opportunity to take a vacation in your brain, diving into another world like diving into a pool, and coming out revived, refreshed and recreated.

If someone sits next to you on your bench, this could evolve into a perfect opportunity for a discussion about books. Strangers always want to know what another is reading. Many is the time that I have started a fascinating conversation with a stranger over books. Enthusiasm for a book is a great way to start a new friendship. There are some books that become a marker for a philosophy of life that may become life-defining. *Jitterbug Perfume* by Tom Robbins is one such book for me – if

It's a perfect opportunity to take a vacation in your brain.

ever I see someone else reading it on the train, tube or aeroplane, I have to accost them. Our eyes meet, we will smile, and we will know that we both share a secret. I am not at liberty to tell you the secret – read the book, then next time we meet, we will smile at each other, knowing that we share something unique.

Reading on the Way Home From Work

As with reading on the way to work, reading on the way back can be vital downtime for restorative escapism into a fictional world. Many of my clients tell me that reading a gripping thriller, a fantasy novel, a romance or literary fiction at this moment is their perfect way of resetting their brain in preparation for coming home. Whether you are returning to a noisy family, a quiet house or have other commitments to rush out to once you get home, spending time reading after work will allow you the opportunity to reconfigure yourself, acting like an airlock between the world of work (outer space) and home (the inner spacecraft), where you can decompress and become the person you enjoy being at home, rather than the person you might be at work. If you travel home on a busy train or bus, tube or tram, let me once again urge you to consider an audiobook. Many a tedious hour can be whiled away with a great book in your ear, even when standing with your chin unintentionally pressed into a random stranger's armpit.

Reading in the Evening

One of the loveliest times to read is in the evening, either on your own or with a partner, friend or child. Most of us who have children love reading to them, and even after they are old enough to read themselves, this is a deeply nourishing tradition to keep going for as long as possible. Bear in mind that this does not always have to be in bed, but can be in a quiet time before supper, or you could even try to persuade your children to read to you while you cook. If you are reading to children in bed, make this as calm and positive a time as possible. By its very nature a bedtime ritual should be calm and positive, but we all have times when we are preoccupied by other things, are worrying about money, a relationship or something that has spilled over from work into home life.

Avoid letting this precious time be spoiled by everyday concerns by setting up your reading to be mindful and calm. Make the reading space as relaxing and tranquil as possible – make sure that no other members of the family are playing loud music, or dashing in and out of the room that you are in. Encourage others in the household to respect this time, remembering their own time as children or younger children, when they would have loved this unique experience. Let them know that now you are reading, and this is a special opportunity during which they should also be quiet, or absent.

Ensure that the place you are reading in is tidy, uncluttered and welcoming. The children being read to can be involved in this too, making their room or the place you like to read an inviting place with low lighting, comfy cushions or rugs to sit on, and even nice smells to waft around. You and your children may want to develop reading-aloud rituals, such as lighting a certain candle before you begin, or having a particular rug that you nestle under. Even if your reading can't be done every night, this cosy time will be remembered for ever

Special Places to Read

You may have a reading nook that you go and snuggle in, or a throne-like chair that you like to read from. I know one mother and son who always read in a hammock, one at each end, toes interlocked, where they can both feel weightless, and the hammock is positioned near a window so that the son can look outside while his mother reads.

I know another family in which the father has created a pod in the shape of an egg, where he can read to his small children. Some parents manage to fit under a high cabin bed, in a tented chamber where blankets surround them, and each night they read with a torch.

If you live in a warm climate, a reading tree is another lovely idea. Find a nearby tree with big, comfortable branches. Take blankets outside, some snacks to nibble on and a thermos, and let each member of the family find a nook to recline in. Then take it in turns to read aloud.

and will be a bedrock for happy memories of reading and family time. You can accessorize as much as you like, with fragrant candles, mugs of hot milk or chocolate, a place for the cat or the dog to join in, and you can even bring in the toys as puppets to act out the drama.

Reading Before You Go to Bed

For many the most popular time to read is before bed. It's the end of the day, and time to put the day, as well as your mind, to rest. This is the perfect moment to pick up that book you've been waiting for all day. For some, it's a meditative experience to read books that focus on self-development, or to think about spiritual matters. Spending just ten minutes reading at this time is as good as deep meditation. Nestle under your duvet with a good book, and allow your mind to wander into new territories. This moment between consciousness and unconsciousness is a perfect time to take your mind to the liminal.

A poem could be the perfect end to your day – one you have read and re-read, and might even be learning off by heart. Or it could be that crime thriller you are gripped by, in danger of keeping you up to the early hours. Allow your eyes to saccade gently over the text, and in some cases, this will be the signal for your brain to start calming down, chilling out and switching off. Many people nod off when reading in bed, and listening to audiobooks last thing at night is for some a desirable way to send yourself to sleep. Every reading brain is different – some people won't read at night because they get too hooked into the book, and know that they would be up into the early hours if they allowed themselves to climb into the embrace of the story. Others find that two or three pages sends them sinking deep into Lethe's arms; they only have to allow a few pages of text to drift past their eyes before they find their head upon the pillow. Whatever you do, make sure that you read a little bit every evening, as even a few minutes will slow your heart rate, de-stress you and allow you to be mindful of meditating on the act of reading itself just for a moment before falling asleep.

MINDFULNESS EXERCISE
USE A NOTEBOOK
❋
Turn off the wi-fi for an hour, go to a different place to read than you normally do – up a tree, in a hammock, in a boat – then read. Enjoy the rocking of the boat, the sensation of the sun on your back, the feel of the pages, the grass beneath your feet or the cosy fire in front of you. When you finish reading, pick up a notebook and write down what you felt.
- What did you feel about the book?
- The place you were? Yourself?
- Spend ten minutes writing whatever comes into your head.

Uninterrupted Reading

It's important to make sure that you get regular periods of uninterrupted reading time, when social media and friends will not interfere with you and your reading practice.

Tell friends via a social platform that you will be reading for the next two hours and you can't be interrupted. Then stick to your resolution and switch off the wi-fi. Turn off your phone too and put it in a drawer so you won't be tempted to check it, then get comfy and settle down in your reading nook with your favourite book.

Don't allow any feelings of guilt to enter your mind. This is important brain re-wiring time, and it will benefit you for the rest of the week. You will be refreshed in brain and body, and the balance of your mind will be restored so that whatever stress life throws at you in the ensuing days will be lessened. Household chores, admin and social necessities must be forgotten during this vital, enriching time. Set an alarm if you need to do something important after this mind-spa. If you don't have any pressing engagements afterwards, however, allow the two hours to turn into three.

Listening to Audiobooks

There was a time when audiobooks were difficult to get hold of. In order to listen to a decent audio version of a book, you either had to get an expensive recording, or borrow one from your local library, whose range might be rather limited. Audiobooks were perceived as being exclusively aimed at the blind or very old, and their quality was highly variable.

WE ARE LUCKY TO LIVE in a time of audiobook heaven. Most novels that are printed are also made into audiobooks, almost as a matter of course. Famous Hollywood actors frequently make recordings of bestselling novels, or interesting literary fiction, as a further string to their bow. Audiobooks are the fastest-growing segment in the digital publishing industry. The United States continues to be the biggest market for the audio format, but all around the world, people are also listening to far more audiobooks than ever before. Around thirty per cent more audiobooks are being published every year, and around one in ten people now listen to audiobooks, as opposed to one in fifty twenty years ago.

A Lifestyle Choice

Adults are listening to audiobooks at younger and younger ages too – while twenty years ago they were perceived to be for older people or for those who were visually impaired, they are now becoming more and more of a lifestyle choice. People listen to audiobooks while commuting, while working out at the gym, while running and while cooking, as well as anywhere else you can think of. Children's audio fiction is also popular, but the adult market is where most growth is occurring. Research in the publishing industry suggests that readers choose audiobooks because it enables them to read more – with people living their lives on the go, having an audiobook on your phone is a constant that's reassuring, entertaining, educational and thought-provoking, rather like having a constant friend in your pocket. The fact that audio works when you are offline is also a big plus.

Smartphones have made listening to audiobooks so much easier, and this is partly why they have taken off recently. When I was a child and a teenager, the only way to listen to audiobooks was to use cassette tapes. These were a good option, being small and portable, but many was the time that the car tape-player chewed up Douglas Adams' *The Hitchhiker's Guide to the Galaxy*, or Sherlock Holmes short stories, just at the most exciting part. Then came CDs, which were also portable, but somehow less so than a cassette. Some listeners still use compact discs, which are great in the car, but these days so many people have switched to listening to their music using a smartphone, that CDs are becoming antiquated too. Phones that can be plugged direct into a car-stereo system are particularly useful for this, since you can seamlessly switch from listening on the phone while ironing, to folding up the laundry, to then getting in the car to go to work. For those of us with more ancient cars, we have to resort to the phone in the cup technique, in which the cup amplifies the sound of the audiobook enough that you can hear it over the hum of the spluttering engine . . . Audiobook listeners tend to average about fifteen books a year, but I get through around a hundred. It's interesting to ponder what makes people love audiobooks. A survey of audio listeners came up with the following reasons: they can do other things while listening; they can take the audiobook wherever they go; and they enjoy the sensation of being read to.

Which Audiobooks to Listen To?

If you are new to the world of audiobooks, you could begin with a childhood favourite, such as *The Secret Garden*, *Pippi Longstocking* or *Great Expectations*. If you feel like being more adventurous, think about the books you would like to read. Perhaps you have never read some of the classics, and would like to catch up on a Russian great, *Madame Bovary*, a Hermann Hesse or a Joseph Conrad. If so, don't feel that you have to listen to the entire unabridged work. Many audiobooks are now available either in their full form, or abridged into more manageable sizes. *Bleak House* by Charles Dickens, for instance, is forty-two hours in its unabridged form, but a mere six hours twenty-eight minutes when abridged. In my Cambridge

The Comfort of Being Read To

The pleasure of being read to harks back to our earliest memories of being read to as a child, or even as a baby. Hopefully most readers of this book will have been read to in their childhood and infancy, and will have distant memories of being on their parent's lap or in bed, cosy and safe, listening to a parent's voice. Remembering this will have an instantaneous calming and soothing effect on the listener who is experiencing an audiobook being read to them. The sound of the narrator's voice will send them straight back to that peaceful, happy and comforting place where they have no responsibilities, no troubles, I hope, and no concerns about the next day. Depending on the reader, you will either be instantly transported back to this memory, or if the reader for some reason has a more grating or harsh voice, or one with an unfamiliar accent, you might be actively entertained and energized by the reader, rather than passively enjoying the experience. Whatever happens, I am sure that you will find being read to soothing and comforting, and hopefully it won't be soporific – especially if you are driving. If the reader turns out to have a less soothing voice, turn the tables and read to them instead.

days, I would have balked at the idea of listening to a shortened version of a classic. But now I embrace it. Faced with the daunting task of a forty-two-hour listen, you might never begin, and thus miss out on the treat of meeting the saintly Esther Summerson, the depraved Tulkinghorn and the marvellous Inspector Bucket. *Moby-Dick* by Hermann Melville, is twenty-six hours of listening at its full length, but you can obtain a four-hour version. Many would be appalled that I might suggest an abridgement of the great work, but I feel that it's better to listen to some of it than none. Of course, if you can either read or listen to the whole thing, this would be even better – wherever possible, I am a keen advocate of reading the entire novel – but it could well be that listening to an abridged version will whet your appetite for more.

Once you get into the swing of audiobook listening, you will find that you discover more and more excellent reads, from contemporary novels to those classics you want to get under your belt. You may find that you respond particularly well to certain voices, and that you want to keep going back to particular narrators. Some genres of audiobook will work better for you than others – perhaps crime, or comedy suits you, while you would rather read literary fiction or narrative non-fiction in book form. The activity you do while listening may also dictate the kinds of books that work best for you – you might like a fast-paced thriller for going to the gym, but a gentle romantic novel for doing the housework. Elizabeth von Arnim on audio would be great for gardening to, and Laura Esquivel is perfect for cooking. Some books are great for sharing, and listening to with your partner or family, such as the Harry Potter series or *Journey to the West (Monkey)* by Wu Cheng'en, while others are just for you, such as *The Old Man and the Sea* by Ernest Hemingway. Whatever suits you, embrace listening to audiobooks, as this will take you on new flights of fancy in your reading and allow you other ways to escape into the world of books.

READING WHILE DOING OTHER THINGS

For some people, sitting and reading can be simply too static. Children with ADHD, for instance, find sitting still almost impossible, so reading in itself feels like a stultifying activity. Many adults also want to be on the move, using their body, hands or feet all the time. This can mean that reading is an alien activity to them. They need to find a way of moving while they read. There are various ways of tackling this, and one of them is to do something else while reading.

Hula Hoop and Read

This is one of the easiest and most successful reading 'hacks': obtain a hula hoop. I have one that you can take apart into segments, which means I can take it wherever I go. Snap it back together, and it has a great weight to it. You can get differently weighted hoops for different intensities of exercise. If you want to really go for it, find a heavier hula. If you just want to be doing something while reading, use one that's a bit lighter, around 1kg. If you're not a regular hula-hooper, then using a medium-heavy hoop is a good idea – heavier hoops are easier to get going than lighter ones, but when they are too heavy, they are more demanding to use. Hold your book in one hand and use the other to set the hula going. Then hula for as long as you like. I normally do about twenty minutes at the end of the day, but I have been known to hula for hours. My daughters like to hula, read and walk at the same time. Don't try this unless you are a highly professional hula-hooper-reader!

Read in a Tree
Search out a beautiful tree that speaks to you with its scale, beauty or personality. Trees draw people to them, and some speak to us more than others – many of us have experienced powerful connections with trees, and feel a need to visit them frequently. If you are lucky enough to have one in your garden that has a suitable branch to sit in, make that your reading tree. Otherwise, explore your local park or woodland, and find a tree that will lend itself to sitting in. Then, when you next have a half hour or more to spare, take your book to the tree. Wear clothes that will be comfortable for climbing in and take a cushion or rug with you.

Ascend into the arms of the tree, and find yourself a lovely nook to sit on. Rest your head against the trunk. Feel the bark of the tree. Smell its unique arboreal aroma. Breathe in its oxygen. Now read for as long as you can. Periodically take time to look away from the text, and while you think about what you have read, gaze up at the sky through the canopy of leaves. Revel in its dancing, ever-changing greens. Perhaps it is spring, and you are sitting in the nook of a cherry tree – you can look up through the wonderful blossom. Or it is autumn, and the leaves are turning yellow, orange or gold. Enjoy the multitude of colours,

You will discover a memory palace of a natural and organic kind.

and project your thoughts about your book onto the canopy of leaves. What would the characters in your novel be thinking if they were in this tree? If you are reading non-fiction, try to place ideas in the tree. Put some ideas into one branch, some others into the canopy and yet more into the roots.

You will find this process helps your memory – when you next think about the book and what it has taught you, visualize your reading tree. Think of what ideas you placed in the canopy, which you placed in the roots and so on. You will discover a memory palace of a natural and organic kind.

If you are reading about history, think about the age of the tree you are sitting in. Could the tree have been alive in the time of the events described in your book? Imagine what might have happened around it.

MINDFULNESS EXERCISE

PRACTISE YOGA WHILE YOU READ

✳

Sphinx pose

Lie down with your belly on the floor, then raise your back and neck up, placing your elbows on the floor beneath your shoulders and stretching out your toes. This is a perfect position in which to read – place the book between your hands, or use a bookstand placed at optimum reading distance from your head. You can remain in this pose for as long as you like – I recommend about ten minutes, then move on to the next yoga-read pose.

Legs up the wall

This is a lovely pose for reading in. Find a space in your house where there is room for you to lie down next to a wall, with your bottom at the base of the wall and your legs going up straight towards the ceiling. Doors between rooms can work well for this, as long as no one is about to burst through them. Sit down, then shimmy your bottom up to the edge of the wall. Reach your legs up the wall or door until they are straightened out. Hold your book at arm's length, with both hands. Read for at least ten minutes.

Lotus pose

This is a more challenging yoga pose, but can be done in a modified form to make it easier or more difficult. Sit down, then extend both feet out from your hips, in a V-shape. Now bring both heels towards your pubic bone, crossing over each other until you find yourself in a lotus pose. If you are not accustomed to this position, you can achieve a half-lotus pose quite easily. The feet can come to rest on the thigh. Now, with a straight back, begin to read your book. Breathe in and out slowly, enjoying the position and remaining mindful of your body while you read.

Child's pose

This is one of the easiest and most instinctive yoga poses. Kneel down on a mat or towel. Put your heels under your bottom, then lean your head over your knees and stretch your hands out in front of you. For a moment, close your eyes and enjoy the sensation of being curled up in your own body and head. Now pick up your book or e-reader, and read, holding both arms stretched in front of you. Hold the pose for at least ten minutes.

Frog pose

Kneel down on the floor, then take your knees out further. Take them as far as is comfortable, with a little bit of extra space, pushing them beyond a limit that seems natural to you. The aim of this pose is to open up your hips and alleviate back pain. Place your elbows underneath your shoulders, and allow your hands to relax on the floor. Read for at least five minutes.

Supine twist

Lie down on your back with legs extended. Bend one knee and cross it outside of the opposite foot, so that your leg crosses the other one. Keep your shoulders squared and rooted to the floor. Extend the opposite hand and put your book or e-book in it. Read for five minutes, then do the same with opposite leg.

Downward-facing dog

Get onto the floor on your hands and knees. Set your knees directly below your hips, and your hands slightly forward of your shoulders. Spread your palms, index fingers parallel or slightly turned out, and turn your toes under. Lift your knees away from the floor, and straighten out your legs. Keep your bottom up in the air. Straighten out your arms. Place your book or e-reader in your eyeline. Keep breathing slowly. Try to do this for five minutes.

Read on a Swing

Remember being a child, sitting on a swing and spending hours enjoying the soft back-and-forth motion of your body in the breeze? Hang a swing in your garden, or in a nearby wood, where it can become a swing for all to use. If you live in the city, you may not feel inclined to swing in a children's playground. In the US, swings are becoming popular for adults, with urban swings for grown-ups appearing in many major cities. Some are only present at festivals, but others are permanent. Search out swings for grown-ups, then take your book down to the park, sit in a swing and read. A swing-seat, of course, is also a marvellous place to rock yourself gently while you read. And if you find one that's designed for two, bring your partner, or you might find that you meet a like-minded reader who enjoys the rocking motion too.

Read on a Boat

It's a perfect, sunny day. You want to be outside, but you also want to read. Find your local waterway – whether it's a lake, a river or a lido. Hire a boat. Row out onto the water, and then drift around in a breeze, gently turning the pages of your book. Enjoy the lovely sound of the water against the wooden boat. If you have a friend, partner or child to accompany you, you can take it in turns to row, while the other one reads. Watch the ripples in the water, and allow your thoughts to ripple out with them. Heaven.

Veloci-read

For more extreme exercise while reading, try reading on a bicycle machine.

Prop the book on the console of your machine. Once you get going with your legs, you should be able to hold the book in both hands while you cycle. Or you may be able to adapt the console to hold your book, with a bit of clever engineering and the use of a bookstand or book-holder.

And yet more extreme – only for the experienced – try reading on a unicycle! Make sure you have lots of space around you, and that you are not likely to crash into other pedestrians, readers or cyclists.

Reading on a unicycle could be considered the ultimate form of mindfulness. One must be in perfect mastery of one's balance, and enter a state of flow in terms of remaining upright, maintaining an ability to keep moving at a fairly minimal rate, while simultaneously reading. One's attention must be focused on the book, but also on one's surroundings, so as not to experience wipeout. Both your inner balance and your outer balance must be in harmony, in the same way that a high level of meditation practice tunes your inner and outer experience to be in balance.

CHAPTER THREE

READING
LIKE A CHILD

Can you remember the joy of reading as a child?
With pure enjoyment, discovering words as if for the
first time, revelling in the print, the paper, the feel and
smell of the book. Rediscover that pure state, and take
yourself back to a time of innocence, enabling you to
use the book as a meditation device.

LEAVE YOUR SCEPTICISM BEHIND

◆

When we read as children, we are blank slates. We have no preconceptions of what a book might be like, what it might be trying to tell us and what we hope to get from it. We open the book ready for a story.

A S ADULTS, WE ALLOW OUR PRECONCEPTIONS to get in the way. The reviews might put us off, or make us sceptical about how brilliant the book really is. The cover design might also lead us to perceive the book in a certain way.

We start reading new books with a certain amount of baggage in our brains. Empty your mind of this baggage. Surrender to the author and their words. Say goodbye to preconceptions. One way to do this is to have a friend or partner give you a book that they think you will like, but with its cover concealed. They could wrap the book in silver foil, brown paper or wrapping paper. They could even cover up the title and author name on the inside as well. That way, no preconceptions can enter your mind. You will have no choice but to dive in, unsullied by critical thoughts.

Don't Believe the Hype

Sometimes we are put off books by the hype that surrounds them, so much so that we avoid reading the book for as long as possible, frequently missing the moment to read it at all. So obstinate can we be that we might miss a masterpiece such as

The Goldfinch by Donna Tartt, simply because everyone raved about it so much. If you have a novel of this category, that everyone is talking about, then one good way of tackling the problem is to alter the book physically. This may seem surprising in a book all about mindfulness, and in a chapter about appreciating the qualities of paper, the smell and the feeling of the printed page, but sometimes one must destroy, in order to create. Take your overhyped book outside. Rub some grass onto the cover, which will have the added benefit of making it smell lovely and grassy. Toss it gently into a benign-looking bush, then pick it up again. Find some earth and massage it into the edges of the paper. This process will rob the book of its glamour and gloss, and bring it down from its pedestal to a more humble state, a place where you can read it in comfort, like meeting an old friend with a few wrinkles, rather than a chic stranger in high heels.

Tackling the Epic

Enormous books can put readers off by their sheer weight and volume. Of course, you can use an e-reader, thus rendering your big fat tome as light as a feather. However, just knowing that the book is thousands of pages long can still deter one, and sometimes it's important to cut the book down to size – literally. If you want to read an epic tale such as *Don Quixote* by Miguel de Cervantes, or *A Suitable Boy* by Vikram Seth, but are put off by the novel's length, then cut it into bite-sized chunks. Yes, really. Purchase a cheap second-hand volume of the book from a charity shop or online, so that you can desecrate one copy, but keep a fair copy unsullied for future reference. Then take a large, sharp knife, and very carefully cut the book up into palatable sections. Choose appropriate places to cut – don't do it randomly, but find natural breaks in the tale – your novel may well come in volumes that suggest places to divide the book. Thus, you can cut up *Remembrance of Things Past* into seven manageable chunks, or cut *War and Peace* into four. Once you have cut up the book, simply read the novel as if it is four consecutive books. Your backpack will be lighter, and you will feel infinitely less daunted by length whenever you pick up the latest section to read.

MINDFULNESS EXERCISE

FEEL THE WEIGHT

✳

Take pleasure in the book's physicality. Caress the pages, smell them and absorb the pleasure of the typeface. Take a moment to ponder the wonder that is type. How was it created? Who invented our alphabet? How did you learn to read? This is a thought process that could take you down a long spiral, like Alice's infinite hole, but just allow yourself a few minutes to think about it. Ponder on the Rosetta Stone, and the three kinds of alphabets on it. Think about your own first experiences of reading. Now start reading.

Going Back to Childhood

◆

One of the loveliest ways to travel in time is to read a book that you first read as a child. There are other ways to time-travel with reading – the WAY that you read can be as important as WHAT you read. As adults, we read in snatched, stolen moments, interrupted by life, woes and worries. As children, we can devote whole days to reading, and read in all kinds of unexpected places. When did you last climb a tree and read a book? Take your inner child by the hand and let him or her be your guide.

Communal Reading

Gather a few friends together to read at the same time, and share your books. These activities will take you back into the mindset you had as a child. That ability to 'lose yourself' in a book, and the extreme intensity of reading that we all remember from being children, will be reactivated by the body memory of climbing into that tree, or lying down on the grass, to read.

Night-time Reading

Reading in bed in adulthood can become a sure way to nod off within a couple of pages. Be mindful of your night-time reading options in order to keep yourself awake and read in a more child-like, absorbed fashion. Take a torch to bed and read under the covers. Yes, this may seem absurd, but try it.

It will take you back to nights of illicit reading when your parents thought you were asleep. Enjoy the addiction of turning over the pages, trying not to wake up your partner as they sleep. Don't tell your children! If they catch you they will be at it too, but maybe if you do catch them at it, turn a blind eye – after all, we want our kids to love reading too.

While you read, be mindful of the magic of the situation. You, an adult, are indulging in the pleasure of reading that you may have forgotten in your grown-up life. You may have spent too much time reading tedious legal documents, academic articles or worthy self-help books. Instead, read a ghost story and enjoy scaring yourself, like you used to as a kid.

Take this to the next level and put a tent in the garden, then read in your sleeping bag, with your torch. Or take your tent to a local forest or field; read a spooky story set in a forest to truly terrify yourself. Just make sure you take a phone and have someone to rescue you if you get too carried away! Or, of course, bring a friend or group of friends. Start a new trend – the ghost-stories in-the-wild club!

'When you read a book as a child,
it becomes a part of your identity in a way that no
other reading in your whole life does.'
KATHLEEN KELLY IN 'YOU'VE GOT MAIL' (1998)

Read in Exciting Places

As adult readers, we often read in boringly predictable places. Remember when you were a child, and you read in all kinds of different spots? Up a tree, in a boat, on the floor under a rug, behind a curtain or door, under the trampoline? On a horse? Take your own reading into new places. At the very least, sit on a park bench during lunch. Get more radical, and find unusual places to read in your garden. Build a bower where you can read and be hidden from the world. Read half-way up the stairs, perched on the landing. Find a local tree where you can sit and read if you don't have one in your own garden, or if you don't have a garden. Find a swimming pool where you can read while sitting on a lilo or in a hoop. Sit on the balcony if you live in a flat, or find a roof garden. If you can, build a tree house. Why should tree houses be just for kids? Think about creating your own reading nook in your house or garden, as described in Chapter One. Add exciting features, such as fairy lights, candles (if it's safe to do so) and interesting aroma-makers. Make your nook as quirky and enticing as possible.

Juggle Your Books

Remember when you were a child and you would have many books on the go at the same time? Not everyone read this way as a child, but many did. You might have had one book that your mum gave you, one from the library, one from Father Christmas, one you had to read for school and maybe one full of facts about animals or aeroplanes. Next to your bed, you might have had a stack of ten books, all of which you were dipping into irregularly. If you were an avid reader then, you would have taken those books on holiday with you too.

As an adult, you may be less of a juggler of books and more inclined to only read one book at a time. Embrace juggling once more! Pick up a murder mystery for moments of pure escapism and thrill. Have a contemplative, philosophical novel to hand, to return to over weeks or months, giving you food for thought. Keep a classic in the stack, so that you work your way through those golden oldies over the years. Then have a modern classic too, one that everyone is reading and you know you must, to keep up with the reading world. Add a graphic novel, a popular-science book and a biography, and you've got a perfect mix to dip into, suiting your mood to the different books available at each moment. Just because you are juggling doesn't mean that you are learning less, and becoming less absorbed, in each book. As long as you give each one your full attention every time you pick it up, you will benefit from each encounter with the book.

MINDFULNESS EXERCISE

THROW CAUTION TO THE WIND

❋

Be irresponsible. Make sure before you start that you have nothing truly pressing or urgent to do. Turn off your wi-fi at source. Now, when you read, you have the possibility of staying up all night. Don't stop at a sensible hour unless you really have to. If you are gripped by the book, stay up until the early hours reading it! To hell with caution and convention. If you really love this book, call in sick the next day and read it! Sometimes reading has to take precedence over life. Don't be niggled by your responsible conscience. Revel in the book. Devour it. Binge read. If there's a sequel, buy it the minute you finish reading.

Read While You Walk

Twenty-first century humans have become adept at using their phones while they do many things that should require their full concentration, such as walking, talking to other people and driving. I am not suggesting that you read a book while conversing with others, as that would be rude, or driving, as that would be foolhardy (though while stationary in a traffic jam, it's a possibility – I have been known to read while stuck on the London Orbital), but reading while walking is definitely doable. Many a time have I walked off a train when I've been gripped in a book, and walked all the way home still reading. Many a tube line has seen me reading both on the tube and up the escalator, all the way to work. Practise reading and walking somewhere safe, then take this skill out onto the streets. You'll inevitably strike up some interesting conversations, and I hope not bump into too many lampposts.

Re-read

As children, many of us read and read the same book, over and over again. We may have demanded that our parents read a book to us, and we slowly drove them mad with repetition. Or we may have had a favourite book that we kept going back to, reading hundreds of times, because it provided adventure, comfort and familiarity. As adults, we tend to do this less, conscious of the hundreds of thousands of books out there to be read. Why read a familiar book, we might think, rather than discover a new one? Go back to a book from your childhood. Pick up that dog-eared favourite, be it an Asterix and Obelix adventure, *Little Women* or *Tales of One Thousand and One Nights*. Read it through once more. This simple act will take you back in time, to the person you were when you first read the book. Suddenly you will be six, eight or ten years old, re-living reading that book for the first time. You will experience the joy of once again being that age, and discovering the book as a new world of wonder. Your adult mind will step back from the experience, and add layers of understanding, criticism and questions to the reading experience, and this in turn will deepen your feelings about the book.

Re-reading is not just about re-discovering old favourites from your past. It's also about re-reading current favourite novels. If you've recently read something that you loved, go back to the beginning and read it again. With your second reading, you will find inner depths that you were previously unaware. New nuances, interpretations and hidden meanings will appear to you on the second reading. Keep this book on a 'favourites' shelf in your room, and re-read it every few months. Every time you go back to it, you will see it in a different light, and discover more not only about the book, but about yourself too.

DROP EVERYTHING AND READ

Make a time every day when you sacrifice all else to reading. When you were a child, it's quite likely that as well as randomly reading books whenever the moment grabbed you, you also had times in your day or week that were just for reading. Last thing at night is an obvious example. But there may have been other times when reading was the only priority and all else came second to it.

MANY ADULTS WHO TALK about not having time to read, suggest that kids are the ones who have all the time in the world. There is an element of truth in that (summer holidays – need I say more?). But it is not necessarily true. Children curling up with a book are deciding consciously not to do something else. Not to watch TV or YouTube, not to chat with a friend, not to build a den, do their homework or make slime. Adults who are not reading are actively choosing to do something else. Every time you pick up your phone to text, check your social media or browse the internet, you could actually be reading a book. Next time you have the urge to reach for your phone, pick up the book you have cleverly placed in your bag instead. Even reading for six minutes will take you to another place, another time, another world.

DEAR Time

Some schools have a moment in the day called 'DEAR' time – Drop Everything And Read. This happens at around 2pm, or near the end of the school day, and the convention is that the children stop whatever they have been doing, pick up a book and read it. This is ideally a book that they have on the go, but if they don't have one handy, they must grab any book, and read it. From personal experience, I know that most children love this time – it is a time for kids to switch off from the hustle and bustle of school, stop feeling that they have to learn something, and walk through the wardrobe of their imagination into another world. They can of course read non-fiction too, and some children prefer to read fact-based books. But whatever they are reading, it's twenty minutes of time away from the school walls, to live temporarily in another world or body.

Try to do this yourself. Declare DEAR time at work! Encourage your co-workers and your boss to embrace DEAR time. Not all employers will agree and it may be impractical in some professions, but they might well find that their work-force is happier, more creative, more productive and more interested and interesting, if DEAR time can happen.

MINDFULNESS EXERCISE

READ IN A STATE OF FLOW

✳

Dive into the text – read mindfully. Allow the words to flow around you, don't concentrate on every word. Enter a Zen-like state of flow where you are unaware of the fact that you are reading at all.

• As part of the adventure of returning to your childhood reading experience, eschew electronic reading, and turn to print rather than the screen.
• Find copies of books that you love in second-hand bookshops or charity shops.
• Choose books whose covers you love, and whose pages feel pleasing to the touch.
• Smell the pages, and enjoy the familiar scent of print on paper. Think about what the smell evokes. Does it remind you of certain books, places, even people?
• As you turn the pages, notice the quality of light, the colour and even the smell of the ink on the page, the way that the spine of your book feels against the palms of your hands.

THE FIFTY-PAGE RULE

◆

Give yourself permission to abandon a book. As children, we often get into the habit of reading an entire book, even if we don't love it. We feel a sense of obligation to the writer, to ourselves and perhaps to our parents, to read the whole thing.

I SUGGEST THAT AS AN ADULT, you allow yourself to get over this sense of obligation, and embrace the fifty-page rule – if you don't like the book after fifty pages, you can give up on it. Fifty pages is long enough to allow yourself to be seduced by good writing, and short enough to not waste too much time if this is not your ideal read. If you decide this book is not for you, there are two options – either to get rid of it entirely, sending it to a charity shop or giving it to a friend, or to set it aside to return to another time. It might be that this book isn't for you right now, but one day it will be your ideal read.

I once tried to read *What I Loved* by Siri Hustvedt, but found that I could not get hooked into it, and had to put it down. About a year later, my mother died, and I happened to pick up the book again. This time, when I read the novel, I became completely captivated and sucked in. I realized that it was because the novel was about grief and mourning. In the story, a child dies, and the parents are left bereft. It's about their grief and their life after his death. Although the novel was about very different circumstances to my own, I found that

the process of shock, grief, anger, acceptance and contemplation was very much the same as what I went through over my mother's passing. In the end, the book was immensely helpful as a kind of manual through grief.

Incidentally, Joan Didion's *The Year of Magical Thinking* is also a book that many people find very helpful as an exploration of grief – but I would suggest that it's not a great book to read if you haven't suffered a bereavement. The analysis is so intense and unswerving that anyone lucky enough to be unaffected by the loss of someone close to them might find it too hard to read.

Returning to a Child-like State

Reading like a child is beneficial in so many ways. Returning to a state of unsullied curiosity, delighted expectation and unashamed pleasure can only be a good thing. Think back to your happiest childhood reading experiences, be they reading with a parent, being read to or taking a book to a secret nook. Take your mind back to that cocooned space, and curl your reading self up like the caterpillar that you once were, nestling in a cosy carapace, before you spread your wings and became a grown-up butterfly. Try to remember all the best things about those reading times – the sense of security, the pleasure of being read to, the bubble of the protective world that you lived in. Then slip back into that state for as long as you can, and enjoy reading a book in this child-like state.

CHAPTER FOUR

SHARE THE JOY OF READING

Reading may seem at first to be a solitary experience, but there are many ways to share a good book, not all of which are immediately obvious. The benefits of reading with others are unexpected and addictive. Mindful sharing of reading is one of the greatest pleasures of life.

WAYS TO SHARE READING

◆

Sharing your reading may seem anathema to an adult who prizes their solitary reading time as precious and personal. But once you try it, I believe you will be hooked, and want to use it as an adjunct to your solo reading experiences. In my opinion, there can be no greater pleasure than reading aloud around a campfire; and there are many other ways to read communally that are just as likely to bring a warm glow to your heart and soul.

THE WAYS OF SHARING BOOKS ARE NUMEROUS, and often unexpected, bringing joy and happiness to those who did not expect to find it in literary form. Reading to yourself is of course an absolute pleasure, and many people love this more than anything. But you don't have to sacrifice your solitary reading time to have the social reading time. Think of it more as an extra way of socializing and sharing your love of reading, so that it's an adjunct rather than a replacement for your own personal reading time.

Some of my own happiest memories are of being read to by my father in the outback of Australia, and in various other settings in Finland, Trinidad and South Africa, as well as the deserts of Iran. Sitting by a camp fire in a dried-up billabong, my father would make a fire, then after supper, we would all sit around the flames and he would read to us from Sherlock Holmes books, the short stories of Saki or tales of Greek mythology. Sometimes we would take turns in reading aloud, and as the sounds of the bush around us crackled, grunted and hummed, we would be transported to other places far away by each other's voices. The sounds of the night would pervade the action of the book, and Sherlock Holmes will now forever be associated with the coughs of the possum and the hoots of the banjo frog; the night-time sounds of cicadas, the dialling tone of red-capped robins, brown falcons and galahs. Shoe-maker frogs tapped gently around us, while we took it in turns to read. These moments of communal reading have given me a lifelong love of sharing books, in whatever way we can.

Reading Aloud Together

Reading aloud with a friend or partner can be romantic, fulfilling, intimate and entertaining. When you read aloud, you give of yourself in a unique and unforgettable way. Both reader and listener are fully aware and mindful of sharing a magical moment.

If you can persuade a friend to read with you, you will have one of the happiest pastimes to return to again and again in your life. My husband and I were lucky enough to read the entire Harry Potter series, from book one to book seven, in a tree in the woods near where we lived. We called the tree the Potter tree, because that's what it became to us. And this was before we had children! Of course we now read Harry Potter to our offspring, but we still read together frequently.

MINDFULNESS EXERCISE

READ ALOUD WITH A FRIEND OR PARTNER

✳

Switch off the wi-fi, find a friend or a partner who is willing to join in, and agree to read a few pages of a book to each other. Ideally, choose a short story or collection of poems. Allow time to ponder the story or poem after you finish reading it. When you read aloud, listen to your voice and enjoy it. Make every word matter. Relish the sounds on your tongue, and make them dramatic and interesting. Try to use arresting sounds, accents and levels of intensity. Whisper at times, and shout at others (if it works with the text). Shouting may not be appropriate with a book about snails, perhaps. But you never know. Make the experience as captivating as possible for the listener.

If you are listening, listen mindfully. Don't just listen to the meaning of the words, but listen to the words themselves. Enjoy their assonance, dissonance and the particular rhythm of the prose. Then allow yourself to get lost in the story or poem, enjoying that sense of comfort and being cared for that you have when being read to.

Focus on your own words, how they flow, how they reach the listener and how they receive them. Focus also on your friend or partner's words, how they deliver them, how they hold the book, how they entertain you with their reading. After reading together for half an hour or more, spend five minutes, writing down what you each liked about the experience. Think about the other person's voice, intonation, attempts to use accents or drama, and also about the same things in your own reading. Contemplate the story or poem they read to you, and how it made you feel. Then share your thoughts with each other and mindfully discuss these ideas, taking care to focus on the positive aspects of the experience as much as possible.

At night, while we wash up, my husband reads aloud to me, following me around the house in a slightly sinister fashion, reading ghost stories and thrillers while I do chores. Or when we're on holiday and the evening is drawing in, we watch the sunset sink while reading a short story, poem or a novel. This is always a uniquely calm, peaceful time, when we seem to be in a bubble of secure complicity.

Reading Silently Together

You can also share your reading by reading silently, but together – as a couple, with friends, as a family – on a picnic, round a fire, in a tent, on sofas at home. Although you are not sharing the text, just the fact of being together and all reading at the same time feels intimate, reassuring and positive. Make sure that everyone has a book. Even a toddler can join in – if they are not reading yet, they will soon catch on to what everyone else is doing, and turn the pages of their book, looking at the pictures, probably not silently, but the fact that they are joining in is what matters. They may want to draw, inspired by the book, and this is something to encourage. One nice adjunct to this is to ask everyone at the end to share a little bit about the book they were reading. This may be too formal a step for some, but for some families it is a great way to get children thinking about what they have read, and trying to explain it to others. This will also make them more mindful of what they are reading at the time.

Read Around a Campfire

Get out a ghost story and pass the book around while you read. For added atmosphere, provide candles; each member of the group can hold a candle to their face, to help them to read and to add a spooky glow. This activity will often lead to making up ghost stories of your own, which is all to the good – everyone needs to collect their thrilling tales from somewhere, and it's ideal to start with reading, then continue onto the oral tradition.

Host a Reading Party

Make friends with the owners of your local bar, and arrange for them to let you all read silently, having drinks while reading. You can theme the evening's beverages around the books you are reading – if it's a Russian novel, drink vodka, if it's French, some fine red wine, if it's *The Great Gatsby*, then cocktails – you could all be reading the same book, as a silent book club, or you could all be reading different novels. Alternatively, befriend someone with a large house, and ask them to host your silent reading salon. Don't talk! Save that for later.

Some hotels around the world have embraced this idea. For almost a decade, people have been gathering in the Fireside Room of the Sorrento Hotel in Seattle, where they read silently in immense armchairs, while waiters bring them cocktails, and a pianist gently tinkles in the background. Start your own reading party . . . and see where it takes you.

Start a Book Club

Having your own book club with a group of friends, colleagues or strangers is increasingly popular, with more than fifty thousand book clubs in the UK alone. This can be a wonderful way to talk about books, to read books that you would not normally discover and to make new friends. Book clubs can be run in many different ways, online, in large groups of thirty or even more, or in small, intimate groups. There are no set rules, but book clubs often work best when one person, a host, takes control, chooses the book and hosts the evening. They might research the background of the book and the author, talk about other books written by that author and encourage other club members to bring food relevant to the book. Sometimes readers might like to read out favourite passages, and then discuss them with the group. It is a good idea to have different members of the group taking it in turns to host the session. Some people like to have a rule that no one in the group can have read the book previously. Others like to bring a few suggestions, then choose one of the options together. Whatever you do, the primary aim should be to enjoy talking about the book, and being together.

Reading in Sync

Develop a 'reading buddy' who reads books at the same time as you. They could be near or far; you can discuss the books on the phone, by Skype or by any way of communicating that works for you. This can work brilliantly as an idea for couples having a long-distance relationship, or siblings, parents and children who may live far away from each other, giving them a shared experience to discuss and come back to over a period of time. Try to start the book at the same time, so that you will be roughly in tandem with your reading progress. Speak once a week or so to let each other know how far you have got. Try to finish the book at roughly the same time too, then talk about the book and see how you both felt about it.

Share Quotes from Books

Sometimes it's enough to share just a quote from a book, rather than the whole thing. It's a good practice while reading to find one key quote in a book that seems to you to be the most resonant, memorable and compelling gem, which you might then share with the world.

This can be done in a variety of ways. You can do it on social media, using Twitter, Instagram, Snapchat or Facebook. Or you can place a chalkboard in a communal area where you work or live, such as in a kitchen in the workplace, or a staff-room in a school, or in the shared lift of an apartment block. Then write the quote from your book on that. Put a new one up whenever you finish a book and encourage other people in the community to do the same. This will set you up to enter into an ongoing dialogue with others about the books they are reading.

Hold a Book-Sharing Party

Invite all your friends and neighbours round, and tell them to bring a book, wrapped up in newspaper. Provide food and drink, and encourage everyone to swap the books randomly. Each person will go home with a new book to read, and they can talk about it later. The guests can also each write a little explanation on a postcard that they put inside the book, about why they love it. That way the recipient will have a little glimpse into what the book means to the person who gave it. They can remain anonymous, or not, as they like.

Release Books 'into the Wild'

A lovely way to share books is by releasing a favourite, loved book into the world, then following where it goes. A movement called 'book crossing' began in the US in 2001, and has since grown worldwide, with books travelling to Amsterdam, Australia, India and many more places. Seven million books have travelled to more than 130 countries since the movement began. The way the system works is that you go to the Book Crossing website, and sign up. You then print out a label to put on your book, and you can follow its progress via the website. Whoever discovers the book will find instructions on the label about how to log the book. Using this method, books have crossed continents and sparked thousands of bookish conversations. A similar scheme was started in the UK, called Book Swap, in which the *Guardian* newspaper encouraged readers to take a photo of a book they were leaving in a random spot in a city, upload it to their website, then wait for it to be found. A sticker inside instructed readers what to do. This movement gathered momentum when a large TV company got behind it and tracked the books. If you start your own book-crossing habit, you will be rewarded by many happy readers discovering your favourite book – and will in turn discover many of your own new reads.

CREATING A STREET LIBRARY

As a reader, you will most likely want to share your love of books with others. Occasionally you will also need to cull your library, as described in Chapter Six. An inspiring way to do this is to build your own mini street library outside your house, where you can put unwanted books, or books that you love so much you want others to discover them too.

A GROWING WORLDWIDE MOVEMENT is bringing street libraries to communities, from big cities such as Sydney and Mumbai to remote rural communities in Finland, Peru and Canada. Not only have these street libraries brought books to people who may not be able to afford them, spreading a love of reading, but they have also brought communities closer together. A mini-library appearing in a street gives opportunities for chatting that is unlike most other street activities, and people you have never met before may well appear at your new creation. Stories have been told about love burgeoning through the medium of a mini-library, when a couple have left each other notes in the books. Strangers will strike up conversations about books, homeless people will be given an opportunity to read and a new community hub will be created. The library can also host events, for example 'library takeovers' where for a week or month, the books focus on a particular subject or theme, such as immigration, ecology, heroism or girl power.

Building Your Street Library

The most aesthetically pleasing route is to make your own out of wood, requiring some carpentry skills, tools and time. If you are not particularly brilliant with DIY, you could enlist a local builder or handyperson willing to help your cause. Most people will be excited by the idea and want to lend a hand, as they will see the benefits to the community they live in – bringing books to children, the elderly and everyone in between, whether they are disadvantaged and on a low income or comfortably affluent – they may want to share a community activity and donate their own books to the cause too. You may well find that you start a trend in your village, town or street, and that mini-libraries start popping up in every direction.

You may need to ask the council first before putting up your library, so make sure that you are putting it in an accept-able spot. Instructions can be found online for you to connect with the international Little Free Library movement. They will send instructions on how to build your mini-library, and they will also register you and your library, so that you can become an official steward. You can make your library in an informal way, of course, with no affiliations, but the Little Free Library movement will send you lots of helpful tips on fundraising, building, sourcing books, getting your commu-nity involved and so on.

If you are less keen on the handmade approach, you could try recycling an old appliance, such as a microwave or fridge. Many examples can be seen online where keen mini-librari-ans have built wonderful little libraries using such items. You must make them safe first, so as to avoid injury or noxious substances found in fridges. But their shelving will be helpful, and it is great to re-use these rather than sending them to the dump. Other great ideas for re-using items would be to use a vintage bread oven, a camping stove, a newspaper dispenser or an old armoir or dresser. A cheap but less beautiful option is to obtain a plastic storage bench, or even a wheelbarrow or bookshelf if you have an indoor area such as a patio, an atrium of a shop, or similar area to put your library. Libraries can be made from birdcages, billycarts wedged in gum trees, doll's houses and microwave ovens. Old cupboards, letterboxes and telephone booths have been converted into little libraries. In Berlin, a street library has been carved into the trunk of a tree. In Bhopal, India, a nine-year-old girl unable to afford a bookshelf or box opened a street library for the disadvantaged by stringing ropes against a wall and hanging books on them. You can make your library anywhere – just use your creative juices and talents, and get other people involved. Local businesses will be delighted to donate money, schools can help spread awareness, and before you know it, you will find yourself taking on a whole new lease of life.

Decorating Your Street Library

If you make your own library, paint it creatively. Get children involved, or paint your own masterpiece on it. Add a sign, saying something to the effect of 'Free books – take a book, lend a book'. If you feel the urge to be a true librarian, tie a notebook to your library in a way that it can be placed inside it, and create columns for name, book and date of when borrowed. If possible, allow space for comments. If people comment on the books they

By creating this mini-library, you will be spreading the joy of mindful reading around your community.

have read, others seeing the comments will want to read the books too. By creating this mini-library, you will be spreading the joy of mindful reading around your community.

CHAPTER FIVE

FIND YOURSELF IN A BOOK

The benefits of reading mindfully, internalizing a book, and making it become a part of you forever, are manifold. As readers we often spend hours, days and weeks absorbing a book, but a year later we may have no memory of that book. Make your reading matter more by remembering what you have read, being mindful of the book in new ways that will make every book you read, count.

SIX-WORD MEMOIRS

◆

In 2006, an online magazine called Smith *began a movement that has since picked up thousands of followers. Larry Smith, founder of the magazine, asked his community of readers to describe their lives in just six words.*

HE HAD BEEN INSPIRED by the legendary tale that Ernest Hemingway was once asked to write a story in six words. This was his response:

'Baby shoes for sale. Never worn.'

Responding to Smith's request, his friends and subscribers sent in short life stories in their hundreds, from the succinct 'Cursed with cancer, blessed with friends' to the agonizing 'I still make coffee for two' to the rousing 'From migrant worker to NASA astronaut' and irreverent 'married by Elvis, divorced by Friday'. And the Six-Word Memoir project was born. Since then, six-word memoirs have spread globally into class-rooms, workshops, churches, spoken word slams, and into every place where people like to play with the written word. Now, as a mindfulness exercise, you can do this too (see page 96). This exercise comes under the umbrella of reading because you are writing as the direct result of reading, in a circular style – you are writing something that you will read

later, and you are writing because you know words from reading. The more you read, the more interesting words you can use, and the better the juxtapositions of words are. Go online at *Smith Magazine* and see examples of many more six-word memoirs, which are under headings of ideas such as Six Words Fresh off the Boat (on immigration), Finding the Bright Side, Going Green, Six Word Survival and so on. The more of these you read, the better your own six-word memoirs will be.

The few minutes that you spend meditating on the book will deepen and sustain your relationship with it forever.

Another way of doing this exercise is to write six-word memoirs of the books that you have read. For instance, if you've just read *Madame Bovary* by Flaubert, you could write: Beautiful romantic loves, spends and dies. Or if you have just read *Great Expectations* by Charles Dickens, you could write: Poor boy, raised up, finds truth. Or if you've just finished *Touching the Void* by Joe Simpson, you could write: Climber cuts rope with friend; survives. And so on.

As with writing the memoir of your last twenty-four hours, this is a mindful act that helps you to find the kernel of meaning at the heart of the book that left its impact with you; and the few minutes that you spend meditating on the book will deepen and sustain your relationship with it forever.

MINDFULNESS EXERCISE

WRITE A SIX-WORD MEMOIR

✳

Choose a moment in your day where you will always be in a predictable place. This could be bedtime as the most obvious choice, or when you first get up in the morning. If you have a lunch-time or coffee-break routine, this could be your moment. Now, sit down with a pen and paper, and write a six-word memoir of the last twenty-four hours. Think of one thing that happened that was important – a conversation, an event or a moment. Then write that down in six words. Here are some examples:

Stayed home sick, best day ever
Yesterday I was a different person
Who invited him to the party?
Monday morning, French toast and espresso

As you will see, your six-word memoir can be on any topic, and it can even simply be a jumble of words:

Fresh cut grass bee sting wind
Blossom cat mulch swing book sing

It does not need to make sense. The important thing is to meditate on the last twenty-four hours of your life in a mindful way, then encapsulate those thoughts in six words. You can play with the words for as long as you like in order to make them more poetic, and to make more sense but you can also throw them down, so to speak, like dice, and see what comes up.

KEEPING A READING JOURNAL

◆

Over the years, I'll bet you've been given many beautiful, slim, hard-backed notebooks by loving friends and relatives. Often those Moleskines or more ornate blank books remain on the shelf, waiting for the perfect opportunity to be broached.

Y OU ARE PUT OFF BY THE VISTA of blank untouched pages, the suggestion that profound thoughts must be honed before you dare put pen to pristine paper.

Now is the time for you to turn one of those empty books into a reading journal. This will be a companion for many years, and ideally it should be small enough to take with you wherever you go. It should always be with you, so that you can jot down thoughts about books whenever you feel like it.

Collating Your Memories

The front of your notebook should be devoted to writing about the books you have just read. Whenever you finish reading a book, this is the moment to pick up your reading journal. In that time of mourning the loss of the book in your life, of bereavement for the characters that you have just spent days, weeks or months living with, of feeling bereft and lost, and perhaps, like a drug addict, immediately seeking the next reading hit – this is the moment to write in your book. Pick up a pen, one that you particularly enjoy writing with. Open the journal. Spend a few moments thinking about the book you have just finished. Did you love it? Did you hate it? Do you wish that the main character hadn't died? Or hadn't got married, or walked off into the sunset alone? Do you wish that you could talk to those characters? Live with them, or have them round for dinner? What was it about them that you loved, or hated? Did any of the characters chime with feelings that you have – did their stories make you think of stories of your own? Perhaps one of the characters lost a loved one, in a way that you have too? Or they experienced a broken heart? Or, they discovered that they are happy to be alone? Did the book give you indigestion, or make you want to go on a cycling adventure around the Himalayas? Allow all these thoughts to wash over you, and let them settle into your mind like leaves on the surface of a lake. Simply allow the blank page in front of you to act as a rippling pool for your memories for a few minutes.

Writing Down Your Memories

Now, pick up a pen that you love. As you hold it above the blank paper, relish the fact that you are going to spend a few minutes more in the company of this book and this author. At the top of the page, write the title of the book you have just read. Next, put down the name of the author. Then, today's date (the date you finished the book). And finally, the place that you were when you read the book. Perhaps you read it

Key Notes for Your Writing Journal

- Title of book

- Author

- Date you finished reading the book

- Place you read it

- Thoughts on the book – narrator, narrative voice, plot, characters, any particular resonance with you as a reader

- Links to other books it reminds you of

- Reflections on the book

---

mostly while on holiday, lying on a beach. Or in a hammock in the garden. Or on your own sofa at home, or in bed. Or on a train to Glasgow, or a plane to Hawaii. Noting down the place you read the book will act as a powerful memory tool, instantly bringing back memories of where you were and what you were doing.

In turn, this will remind you how you felt about the book. As you picture yourself sitting on that train, perhaps looking out of the window at the countryside rushing by, you will remember the feelings of yearning, romance or sudden understanding that occurred in your reading brain. These memories will be mixed with memories of what was happening in your life at the time. You might recall the annoying fellow passenger who crunched crisps too close to your ear, or the colourful old lady you helped with a suitcase. You might remember the reason for your journey – visiting a relative, or setting off on a work assignment. These memories will mingle with the recollections of the book itself.

When you look back on this journal months (or years) later, just those words, for example, '*Girl on a Train* – Paula Hawkins – 13 September 2017, train to Exeter', will bring back a flood of memories – not just of the book, but of what was happening in your life at the time. This in itself makes the writing of the journal worthwhile. But having written down these bare essentials, now you must take a little time to write more. Use the rest of the page, which isn't big, after all – probably only enough space for 100 words or so – to write a little about the book. Jot down the names of the main characters, the major events of the novel and a few thoughts of your own about feelings that you experienced during the reading

---

Using the Back of Your Journal

Use the back of the journal for jotting down the titles and authors of those books that people recommend to you on the hoof – when you are chatting over lunch and a friend raves about a read, or makes a passing remark about a life-changing novel. That way you'll never be stuck for what to read next; just refer to your reading journal for the next idea.

---

of the book. Did you feel great sadness or loss, joy, connection with the protagonists, or irritation with the author? This act of thinking mindfully about the book will help you to cement the story into your brain. The very act of writing on the page is an exercise in mindfulness – as you write the words that conjure up the book, you are compelled to consider mindfully its meaning, the way you felt about it and how the book affected you.

The Feel of the Book

Ponder also the feel of the book – its cover, design, colours and even smell. All of these things will have affected the way you feel about it. Frequently the image on the cover will have a fundamental effect on the way you react to the book. Consider *The Essex Serpent* by Sarah Perry, which has a very tactile cover, showing a sinuous emerald serpent twining itself around the title, a cross between a mosaic and a medieval painting. The cover is such a thing of beauty that when you hold the book, it feels like a rare and precious gift. This makes reading the book seem very special.

If you have read the novel as an e-book, or listened to it on audio, this will also deeply affect the way you experienced the story. If it was a book you listened to, write a little in your journal about the narrator. Did you like the way they read? Was their voice soft, or harsh, clipped or sonorous, light or heavy? Did they have a pleasing accent? Did they send you to sleep or keep you riveted? And if you read the book on a screen, was that experience a good one? Was it your phone, so perhaps interrupted by other things, or was it on a Kindle, so easier to control? Note down in your journal the method of reading, and how this affected your reading pleasure.

If the book you've just read reminded you of other books, either by the same author or another, note that down too.

All of this should only take a few minutes. You don't want to be writing an essay about the book, as you have a life that's busy enough without feeling like you are back at school. But by spending these few more minutes in the company of your book, you will remember it forever in a more profound way. Writing your thoughts has fixed the book in your mind, and when you pick up the journal in years to come and see those crucial reminders, for example '*Me Before You* – Jojo Moyes – Tenerife, October 18' – you will be swept back into your life at that time, and remember a combination of life and reading that will enable you to time travel.

> *By spending these few more minutes in the company of your book, you will remember it forever in a more profound way.*

CREATE A GOLDEN TREASURY

◆

As a mindful reader, a magical and nourishing exercise is to create a 'golden treasury' of your favourite writers, poets and thinkers.

A GOLDEN TREASURY IS AN IDEA that dates back to the nineteenth century and Francis Turner Palgrave, who created one of the most loved books of all time, *The Golden Treasury* of poems from Shakespeare to the present. Palgrave was a British critic, anthologist and poet, who compiled a volume containing what he considered to be the finest poetry in history, from Shakespeare, to Spenser, Wordsworth and Coleridge. Palgrave was a great friend of Tennyson, and legend has it that they read aloud the work of famous poets, deciding to include all the poems that passed muster from the reading-aloud process. Since the first edition, the book has been continually updated and revised, and there have been six new editions under Palgrave's name.

Your task as a mindful reader is to create your own golden treasury of all the books you have loved most in your life. First choose a suitable book to turn into your treasury. Choose a large volume that can cope with having paper stuck into it with glue, the kind of book that you might use for scrapbooking. It could have brown paper as a background, or it could be a ring-binder that will expand happily as you stick things in. Get it as big as you dare so that you can stick a lot in.

Choosing Your Books

Decorate the cover in any style you like, adding the title 'A Golden Treasury'. Then start thinking about what you would like to put in it. What are your favourite books from childhood? If you still have them, browse around your earliest books, and choose the ones you loved the best. Dr Seuss' *Cat in the Hat*, Munro Leaf's *Ferdinand* or Tintin. Take photocopies of your favourite pages, and stick them into your treasury. Now you have made a start, you will be on a roll. You may feel that you simply must put in a picture from a Moomintroll book, with a few favourite lines. Or, even if they gave you nightmares well into adulthood, a short story from *Struwwelpeter* might have to go in. *The Little Prince* by Antoine de Saint-Exupéry, *Journey to the West* (*Monkey*) by Wu Cheng'en or *Pinocchio* by Carlo Collodi, may all need a cutting.

Having started on your Treasury, take a bit of time (perhaps a weekend) to look through your books and decide which are the most memorable, significant and emotionally enriching passages in all of these titles. Make copies or transcribe quotes from each of these volumes. You could find about one hundred of them, or more, from over the course of your life so far. They can be poems or prose, a page or two, or just a small quote. These can be children's books such as *Treasure Island* or *The One Hundred and One Dalmations*, Harry Potter or Pippi Longstocking, poetry you read as a child or teen such as Wordsworth's 'Daffodils' or 'El Gallo de Bodas' or Korney

Chukovsky's 'The Crocodile' – as well as important books you read in your adulthood and up to the present day. The key is that you should choose passages from these books, then photocopy them and stick them into an album, or write them out in longhand.

Decorating the Treasury

Decorate the pages with your own illustrations, or with pictures from magazines, wrapping paper, craft paper or anything that takes your fancy (see page 106 for ideas). Put time and love into this project, choosing paper, paints, colours and textures that you will delight in over the years. Whenever you go back to this Treasury in the future, you will remember choosing those papers and the act of creation, and this will feed back into the love of the stories and poems, extracts and quotations that you have chosen.

Find different ways of presenting the extracts on the page. Some could be written on white paper, others could be white pen on black, or copies that are then stuck onto brown paper. You could even print onto acetate, and have a poem, passage or quote overlaying another one. Once you have chosen all your passages, spend an afternoon sticking them in your Treasury, and another afternoon decorating them. This is a project that could take a few weekends, or evenings. But once it is created, you will find that you want to keep going, and now whenever you read a book or a poem, or hear something

Decorating Ideas

Decorate your cover in an imaginative style. Cover the book with velvet or recycled fabric. Visit your local charity shop for materials – use tapestry, leather or suede to create a textured cover. You could embroider the title on the front.

Decorate the pages too. You could include quotes from the books, written out in hand, or you could type them out and then stick in the printed excerpts. Attach ribbon, in pure colours or patterns, in whatever style suits you best. Get some tips for decorating by searching scrapbooking forums online. You could use maps as backgrounds, placing your book in a particular place, the location of the story or where you read the book. Use buttons, add collage from magazines or newspapers to create interesting areas on your page, or get out brushes and paints to make your own images. Illustrate the passages with pictures borrowed from the books themselves, or ones that you have made up yourself. If you are good with a sewing machine, you could experiment by sewing your poems, samples of books and quotes onto the page. For the truly nifty with a needle, you could even write whole passages with needle and thread. Discover the joys of washi tape, which is a decorative masking tape that you can use for sticking in passages to your Treasury, for creating borders around the page, or simply making pleasing patterns.

on an audiobook that you can note down, you will want to put it into your Golden Treasury. You will find yourself poring over it constantly, reading through the old passages, and relishing the new ones.

A Seasonal Treasury

A twist on this idea is to make a seasonal version of the Treasury. Divide a large scrapbook into four sections, and label each section with a front page – Winter, Spring, Summer and Autumn. Decorate the front pages with seasonal themes, use the colours of each season – draw leaves, or stick them in, or simply paint the whole page in one colour.

Then go through your books picking out passages that you love that relate to the different seasons. Select poems that characterize the seasons, such as 'To Autumn' by John Keats, or Robert Frost's 'Stopping by Woods on a Snowy Evening'. Then, think of the books you have read that evoke a season. *Snow* by Maxence Fermine is a beautiful book about haiku, snowflakes and tightrope walking. *The Ice Palace* by Tarjei Vesaas is a melancholic, haunting novel about a palace of ice created by a waterfall. Tove Jansson's *Moominland Midwinter* gives us a moomintroll waking up early from his hibernation, and exploring the snowy world around him. All these would make lovely entries into a seasonal Treasury, but of course you will have your own favourite extracts that will be perfect ones for your scrapbook.

Read Real Books

Many of us have embraced the joys of the e-reader, and it is indeed an excellent way of making books portable. E-readers have transformed the lives of students, travellers and extreme readers, and I am a big fan of them. However, some studies by neuroscientists have shown that reading on-screen can be less memorable in the long term than reading 'real' books. They say that the brain is not wired to 'believe' in a page that has disappeared from tangible reality. Once you flick the page away, it disappears and effectively does not exist in a touchable, graspable way. With a printed book, the page is still there, you can feel it, turn back to it, and hold it in your mind. With e-readers, once you have read the page, it disappears until you call it back. Your brain is not designed to hold on to the reality of this page, and therefore does not remember it so well as with a 'real' page. If reading on-screen is a necessity, there are ways to make it more mindful. Love your device – touch it and smell it, cover it with a beautiful case. Enjoy the text size – make it bigger or smaller to suit you. Try to regularly browse your 'library' of books on your e-reader, and delete those you no longer need, in the same way that you would cull a palpable library. Seeing the books that you have on your device will help you to remember which books you have read, and which are waiting to be read.

Write out whole poems, choose extracts from novels, print short stories that will fit into your book. Include nonfiction if you find particularly powerful descriptions of seasons in other kinds of books, such as *Touching the Void* by Joe Simpson, which has wonderful descriptions of mountains in the snow, or for the summer, look at desert-themed books such as *The Map of Love* by Ahdaf Soueif, which will fill your mind with images of heat and sand.

You can spend many happy hours creating this seasonal Treasury, and then every time the seasons turn, enjoy leafing through your wonderful collection of seasonal literature.

RE-READING

Re-reading books can be as good, or better, than reading a new book. Throughout my life, I have read and re-read books, loving the process of returning to books again and again. In childhood, one can re-read almost infinitely, but this is a different kind of process, linked to the very act of learning to read.

I'M NOT TALKING ABOUT THAT HABIT of reading the same book every night to the point of driving your parents insane (especially if they are the ones reading the book to you in the first place), but that conscious pleasure of going back to a book that you read in childhood, formative teenage years or as a young adult.

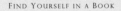

MINDFULNESS EXERCISE

PAY MORE ATTENTION TO LANGUAGE THAN USUAL

✳

Pay attention to language as you read. Look at an individual word; look up unfamiliar words in the dictionary. Maybe use a pencil to underline language that you notice, or just make a mental note. Either way, get into the details – the rhythm of a sentence, a word that conjures a person or place. Notice if reading causes your thoughts to meander. Your mind is not a vacuum sweeping up each word mechanically. You will invariably drift off, that is natural. But focusing on each word will help you to overcome a tendency to skim – make yourself engage with each word on the page, and then on one whole page at a time. See the book as something that comes in bite-sized chunks – words, paragraphs, pages, chapters. This way the book as a whole will seem so daunting.

Stop reading once on every page for ten to thirty seconds. When you pause, meditate mindfully on the last thing you read. Read this passage from Wordsworth's 'Intimations of Immortality' as an example:

'There was a time when meadow, grove, and stream,
The earth, and every common sight,
To me did seem
Apparelled in celestial light,
The glory and the freshness of a dream.
It is not now as it hath been of yore –
Turn wheresoe'er I may,
By night or day,
The things which I have seen I now can see no more.'

Stop when you reach any word that grabs your attention, for instance 'celestial'. Now think mindfully about that word. Say it inside your head. Think about the sound of it, the repeated 's', and consider what it means. What associations does it bring? Meditate on the word, remembering where you

have heard it elsewhere, in what context you might use the word yourself and whether you can bring it into conversation today. Look it up in the dictionary. The definition of 'a celestial body' is generally 'positioned in or relating to the sky, or outer space as observed in astronomy'. You may find many similar words listed: space, heavenly, astronomical, extraterrestrial, stellar, planetary, in the sky, in the heavens, holy, saintly, divine, godly, god-like, ethereal, paradisical, Elysian, spiritual, empyrean, superlunary.

Enjoy all these new words: heavenly, astronomical, extraterrestrial, stellar, planetary, ethereal, superlunary. Roll these words around your mouth, and imagine using each of them. 'My heavenly husband', 'that ethereal mist', 'that paradisical wine'. Jot them down in a notebook, or on your phone, so that you will remember the words and use them again. Then, later that day when you are talking to a friend, try to slip the word into your conversation. 'You are looking celestial', you might say. 'That concert was stellar.' You will enjoy adding new words to your vocabulary, and you will also deepen your relationship with your reading. If you do this exercise only once each time you read, you will add one new word to your vocabulary every day, enriching your conversation and expanding your mind.

Revisiting an Old Favourite

Re-reading is also a kind of security. By going back to a book that you read as a child, you can return to a place of safety, comfort and lack of responsibility.

Picking up a book that you read in your teens or childhood is an act of time travel. The moment you start reading to yourself, you will be transported back to the days in which you first read that book. Going back to *Tess of the D'Urbervilles* by Thomas Hardy, for instance, is for me a revisit to myself as a fifteen-year-old girl. When I first read the story of Tess, I was at school, reading it during an English lesson. I found it deeply romantic and tragic. Tess was an innocent, seduced and tricked by Alec D'Urberville, who seduced her in the forest, and then left her pregnant. She had believed in him at first, but was then effectively ruined by him. I had total sympathy for her, and found her vulnerable state very moving.

Re-evaluating

When I returned to the book a few years later, I found Tess passive, naive and annoyingly accepting of her fate. I wanted to shake her up and tell her to become the mistress of her own destiny. This was probably because I was beginning to feel like I did not need to float on the stream of life like flotsam, but could decide my own fate. I noticed the change in my feelings about the book, and realized how my own character had changed since that first reading.

Then, re-reading the book in my thirties, I felt differently about Tess yet again. I still had the two layers of experience of reading the book – my first, in which I was swept up by events, desperate to know what would happen to the heroine, living her agony and feeling entirely sympathetic to her plight – my second, in which I knew the unfolding of the drama, but was curious about how and why Tess made her decisions, and was far more critical of her – and now, my third layer of reading and understanding was far more sympathetic to Tess' experiences. I put the character back into the context of the time she lived in, realizing that she was a victim of circumstance, society and the expectations of women of her time. I was still annoyed by her passivity, but began to feel more sympathetic again.

A fourth reading a few years later put me even more in a state of sympathy for Tess, realizing that she does indeed take control of her own destiny as much as she can.

New Insights

Every time I re-read Hardy's novel, I find more details and insights within the text that I love – things I had not noticed before, even when studying the book's plots, motifs and themes extensively.

The joy of reading and re-reading is that there are always new details that will call out to you to be noticed and mulled over. For instance, consider this passage:

'The gray half-tones of daybreak are not the gray half-tones of the day's close, though the degree of their shade may be the same. In the twilight of the morning, light seems active, darkness passive; in the twilight of evening it is the darkness which is active and crescent, and the light which is the drowsy reverse. Being so often – possibly not always by chance – the first two persons to get up at the dairy-house, they seemed to themselves the first persons up of all the world. In these early days of her residence here Tess did not skim, but went out of doors at once after rising, where he was generally awaiting her. The spectral, half-compounded, aqueous light which pervaded the open mead impressed them with a feeling of isolation, as if they were Adam and Eve. At this dim inceptive stage of the day Tess seemed to Clare to exhibit a dignified largeness both of disposition and physique, an almost regnant power, possibly because he knew that at that preternatural time hardly any woman so well endowed in person as she was likely to be walking in the open air within the boundaries of his horizon; very few in all England. Fair women are usually asleep at mid-summer dawns. She was close at hand, and the rest were nowhere.

'The mixed, singular, luminous gloom in which they walked along together to the spot where the cows lay often made him think of the Resurrection hour. He little thought that the Magdalen might be at his side. Whilst all the landscape was in neutral shade his companion's face, which was

MINDFULNESS EXERCISE

PONDER ON A PAGE

✳

Read a whole page, being aware of every single word. Choose one of your favourite novels, one that has had resonance and which you remember partly for its use of language. *Lolita* by Vladimir Nabokov could be a great example, or *On the Road* by Jack Kerouac.

Read the first page of the novel. Say it aloud in your head. Turn it over on your tongue. Put it into the whole sentence. When you get to the end, re-read the same page again, this time allowing the words to flow. The first exercise will have made you fall in love with each word, the second will make you fall in love with the narrator or narrative.

At the end of the second reading, pause for a few moments to reflect on the page you have just read. How did it make you feel? Make a note at the bottom of the page. Yes – it's OK to write on a book. Did the passage make you feel happy, sad, thoughtful, reflective, did it strike a chord with your life?

Think about a few ideas that might resonate with you. Have you experienced anything like this in your own life? Spend a few minutes remembering, be it good or bad. If it is an unhappy memory, think about the good things that have happened since then. If it is a good memory, think about the similar experiences that have made you happy.

Think about the words themselves. Are there any unusual words that you don't use often in your vocabulary? Write them down on a notepad or on your phone, and try to use those words in your speech today.

Think about the characters. Do you know any people in your own life like those in the novel? If so, what role do they play in your life? Are they a positive or negative influence? If you put these real characters into the novel of your life, what would happen to them? Have a bit of fun while you ponder this idea. Consider writing your own short story, fictionalizing the characters in your own life.

the focus of his eyes, rising above the mist stratum, seemed to have a sort of phosphorescence upon it. She looked ghostly, as if she were merely a soul at large. In reality her face, without appearing to do so, had caught the cold gleam of day from the north-east; his own face, though he did not think of it, wore the same aspect to her. It was then, as has been said, that she impressed him most deeply. She was no longer the milkmaid, but a visionary essence of woman – a whole sex condensed into one typical form. He called her Artemis, Demeter, and other fanciful names half teasingly, which she did not like because she did not understand them.'

Experience the Description

The idea that Hardy encapsulates in his description of dawn, in which 'light seems active, darkness passive', gives us a wonderful observation of a natural phenomena, imbued with a typically Hardy-esque vision that overlays the mysterious light of dawn with an intention, that of daylight overpowering the night, just as at night-time, darkness overpowers the day.

As an exercise, try sitting in a comfortable place outdoors in the gloaming so you can feel that presence of darkness that overpowers the light. While you sit, be conscious of your breathing, your body posture, your place on the planet. Try to notice everything – look at the effects around you as the light is slowly drained from the sky, and the colours around you turn from green and blue to a symphony of greys. Ponder what Hardy was talking about – the 'gray half-tones of the day's close', which are not the same as the 'gray half-tones of daybreak'. Do you feel a sense of the active nature of darkness? If you do, think of ways to describe it yourself. Have a notebook to hand, and jot down words and phrases that come to mind. Listen to the sounds around you and note them down too. Smell the air, feel the ground you are sitting on, the branches and leaves or grass around you, and think about the sensations you are experiencing.

Repeat the Exercise

Now contrast this to your experience of dawn. Set your alarm for fifteen minutes before dawn, then get up and, with a cup of peppermint tea or hot water, go outside and watch the slow changes in colour and atmosphere around you. As with the dusk exercise, sit somewhere comfortable, and centre yourself in your body. Breathe in and out deeply with your eyes closed, thinking about your breath. Now open your eyes and watch the slow change from darkness to light. Does the light itself seem active, and the darkness passive? How can you describe this? Jot down in your notebook anything you notice, from changes in colour, to changes in the density of light and the sharpness of definition. Listen to the waking world, and jot down words and phrases that come to mind. Smell the air, observing the differences between the dusk air and the dawn. Watch the shadows changing around you, and

MINDFULNESS EXERCISE

RE-READ AN OLD FAVOURITE

❋

Go into your book collection and choose an old book that you loved as a child. If you don't still have a copy, find one in a bookshop, library or borrow a copy from a friend or relative. In this instance, I would urge you to make sure you get a real copy of the book, rather than an e-book. The experience of holding the book in your hands will be important; the smell of the pages, the feel of the paper and the memories triggered by the cover will resonate with you far more strongly if the book is a physical object, not on a screen. Pictures will be extremely powerful, and if you have the original book from your childhood, the texture and aroma will be very suggestive. I, for example, have a copy of Munro Leaf's *Ferdinand*, which is the actual book that I had as a child. The pages are yellowed with age, the spine is falling apart, but the words and pictures are still just the same. I coloured in the pictures with crayons, and I can remember doing it. You may have stains and scribbles on your own old books, which will bring back memories of the first place you read them – on your father's lap, or in a cosy spot in your childhood bed-room, or swinging from a tree. Picking up this book and thinking back to when you first read it will take you straight back to a time of carefree read-ing, I hope, to a time when nothing was a worry, and nothing would stop you from reading all day. You will instantly feel that sense of security, of being hugged in the embrace of a parent, or of lying in your childhood bed or holed up in your den.

The book need not be an early childhood read, it could be from your teens or young adulthood. But I would urge you to use a comforting book for this process – not a horror book or ghost story, not a book that is challenging and controversial, but one that guarantees happy endings, nurture and positivity.

revel in the gradual saturation of colour into a world that started off monochrome. You may wish to sketch your surroundings while you watch, as this is also a great way to be mindful and to ensure that you notice things.

COMFORT READS

Without realizing it, we all have comfort reads on our shelves. These are the books that we turn to in times of trouble, or when we are simply exhausted and need cheering up for whatever reason. Most likely, they come from childhood, but a comfort read could also be any old, familiar book that stands the test of time and can be read and re-read, or simply dipped into as a salve for the soul.

MY COMFORT READ WOULD BE *Finn Family Moomintroll*. I first read it when my family lived in Finland, as my father was a diplomat in Helsinki. I was introduced to the Moomins by my mother, who was a major fan. These magical creatures are miniature trolls, small enough for five to fit on a forest floor leaf. Unseen by humans, they nonetheless have very human characteristics, from fretting over the unknown, to worrying about comets coming, having OCD, spending all their time writing their own memoirs, and providing food for the household. Magical events happen in their world; a Groke comes to visit them, spreading ice and loneliness wherever she goes, and natural disasters occur too, such as floods and comets. But Moominmamma is always there with her handbag and a sandwich, Moominpappa can be relied upon to smoke his pipe and wear his top hat, Snufkin will always appear at the beginning of spring, and all little creatures will be welcomed into the Moomin household.

I was delighted by these stories from a young age, Tove Jansson's illustrations being just as entrancing as the words she wrote. Jansson wrote as much for the adults as the children in her readership, delivering humorous descriptions of the foibles of human nature. Thus, whenever I have a moment of worry or sadness, the Moomin books are my go-to comfort read – even if I just pick one up off the shelf and have a quick flick through the pictures, or come across a favourite passage, that will be enough to re-align my consciousness and take me back to a happier and more reliable time of my life. Even simply thinking about the books has the same effect.

Calming Books

Do you have an equivalent? Take time to think about this. Then make sure that you always can put your hands on that book in moments of uncertainty.

To expand more on this idea of a comfort read, set aside a moment to think about what book you would like to have with you if an emergency arose, if you were stuck at the bottom of a well for three days, for example, or if there was an earthquake and you were caught under a table awaiting

MINDFULNESS EXERCISE

FINDING YOUR COMFORT READ

✳

What would be your comfort read? Take a moment to ponder this and write down a few possibilities.

Think back to your childhood and teens. Did you have books that you perhaps unconsciously picked up at times of need? Books that you loved, without really thinking why? It might have been a picture book, one that you loved first because of the visual element, which you first saw when you were very young – a book by Beatrix Potter, Dr Seuss or Maurice Sendak, perhaps. Or it might be a book that you first read to yourself, and got lost in a story in the way that is so unusual to experience as a grown-up.

If you can remember such a book, picture it in your hands, and imagine turning the pages. Think about the way the book makes you feel. Does it take you back to a carefree place of comfort and safety? Hold that book in your imagination for a few minutes. Remember the story it told, and try to tell it to yourself now.

If you can't think of such a book, go to your bookshelves, and choose the book that appeals to you most in terms of familiarity. Pick it up, hold it in your hands and take yourself into its story. You don't have to open it – just remember it, and tell the story to yourself in your head. This will slowly help you to feel calm, safe and in a familiar world.

rescue. Don't send yourself into an anxiety spin, but use this as an exercise in thinking deeply about what kind of book would keep you calm in such a situation.

It could be poetry, a religious tome, or philosophical musings. It could be ancient wisdom, a collection of haiku or some kind of non-fiction – something that connects you with nature, or maybe you take refuge in science or mathematics. There may be more than one book that would be your ideal volume for such circumstances, but hone down your thoughts into having one book available.

Use this as an exercise in thinking deeply about what kind of book would keep you calm in such a situation.

Now think of a way of having this book with you at all times. You don't literally have to carry it around with you, but you could have a part of it. You could download it onto your phone or e-reader, or keep some pages in your wallet or purse. Better still, learn portions of it off by heart. Feats of memory greater than learning one book have been known. Think of the characters in *Fahrenheit 451* by Ray Bradbury. In their dystopian world, where no books are allowed and all books have been burnt, the rebellious few have each learnt a book by heart, so that they can re-write them at a suitable opportunity. In your case, you could simply learn a few favourite poems, or learn whole chapters off by heart.

MEMORIZING PASSAGES & POEMS

◆

It can be a wonderful, nourishing and mindful enrichment of your life to memorize passages from literature, poems and quotations. This is a habit best begun in childhood, but it is never too late to start.

THE PROCESS HELPS YOU TO BUILD UP your memory, gives you natural rhythms to fall back on, gives you a safe haven to go to at times of stress and keeps the 'muscles' of your brain exercised. Choose poems that you knew in childhood, such as 'The Owl and the Pussycat' by Edward Lear, Spike Milligan's nonsense verse, Shakespeare's sonnets or the poetry of Hafez. Whatever you choose, choose it because you love it, you would like to hold it in your heart and you know that you will always be happy to recite it either internally or to a listener. Then repeat the poem over and over again aloud, and in your head, until you have it 'by heart'. The phrase 'by heart' is rightly used, as a poem or passage that you know this well becomes part of your body, part of your very soul, never to leave you; it is the life-blood of your heart indeed.

It can be immensely important, nourishing and resonating to have passages from literature, poems or novels memorized in your head. Brian Keenan, a captive in Beirut for four and a half years, recalls how he re-wrote *Robinson Crusoe* when he was stuck in his cell. In his memoir *An Evil Cradling*, Keenan wrote that the foam mattress in his cell became for him a flimsy raft in an endless ocean. All around him was water, with not a hint of land, giving him no glimmer of hope. He felt as if stranded on a makeshift boat, at the mercy of the elements. In his mind's eye he pictured dolphins swimming alongside his vessel, who rose above the surface and gazed at him eye to eye. He saw other creatures too, and he felt a desire to throw himself off his imaginary raft into the depths of the sea to join them. He would become aware of his true helplessness, stuck without food, water or hope, just like Daniel Defoe's hero. Picturing himself in the same circumstances helped Keenan to survive his solitude.

Learning literature by heart is a way of making the book a part of you forever, alchemizing it into something integral to you and your life. Sometimes a piece of literature can alter the course of a person's life, if discovered at the right moment. Keenan was saved by the books that he knew already, but I would now like to share with you the story of a man who was saved by literature when in a similar situation to Keenan's, but in this case, it was a work that was new to him.

The Story of Mohamed Barud Ali

Mohamed Barud Ali was a Somalian prisoner, placed in solitary confinement in a state prison for complaining about the state of the local hospital. Mohamed had to live in total silence, and in complete solitude. All speech was forbidden; only pacing was a possible activity. Mohamed was sentenced to life imprisonment, aged thirty-four, and his wife was then twenty years old. The government encourages wives to divorce their husbands if they are in prison, and Mohamed's wife had no idea when he would be released, if ever. Mohamed began to go mad in his solitary confinement, blaming his wife for his being in prison; it was on her behalf that he complained about the state of the local hospital. But then one day, a new inmate, named Adan Abokor, coincidentally a doctor from the very hospital that Mohamed had complained about, moved into the cell next door.

Talking in Code

One day Mohamed heard a whisper through the wall: 'learn ABC through wall'. At first Mohamed had no idea what he was talking about, but then Adan, the doctor, knocked on the wall – once for A, twice for B and so on – teaching Mohamed a Morse code of knocks. Then, one day when Adan was given a change of clothes by a guard, he asked the guard for a book. He was given *Anna Karenina* by Leo Tolstoy. Adan began to tap out the book to Mohamed, every single letter on the first of the eight hundred pages of the book. Painstakingly, Adan told Mohamed the story, in Tolstoy's words, letter by letter.

◆

'There is no friend as loyal as a book.'

ERNEST HEMINGWAY (1899–1961)

◆

Literary Parallels

Anna Karenina is a nineteenth-century novel about a young Russian noblewoman married to a man much older than herself. She goes to a ball and falls in love with a soldier, Count Vronsky. But instead of having a secret affair like others in her social set, Anna leaves her husband, making her love public. And she's punished. She's isolated and alone. Anna stays in her room, wondering what her lover is up to when he's not with her, a bit like the way Mohamed was wondering what his wife was doing outside the prison walls. Anna is shamed for her love, and Mohamed's wife, Ismahan, was also shamed for her love. If Ismahan did not divorce her husband, she would be looked down on by society for being married to a 'traitor'.

Mohamed learnt to empathize again, understanding his wife's point of view. He wept for Anna Karenina, and he wept for his own wife too.

Through listening to the book, Mohamed learnt to empathize again, understanding his wife's point of view. He wept for Anna Karenina, and he wept for his own wife too. The scales fell from his eyes as he realized that his wife was not to blame for his imprisonment, and that she may well remain faithful to him. Mohamed was released eight years later, and he remains happily married to his wife.

From this true story we can see how experiencing a fictional love affair and its consequences saved a man's sanity when he was in despair, living in what must have seemed eternal darkness. The immense generosity of the neighbouring doctor who spelt out every word of the novel with patience on a Herculaean scale is probably what kept them both going in their most desperate hours. In that dark state, Mohamed must have been mindful of every single letter of every single word, listening with bated breath for the next letter. Hearing this story makes us appreciate our own ability to read freely all the more.

Make books a part of you by internalizing them when you read them. Being more mindful of your reading habits will help you to grapple the book to you with hoops of steel, like a best friend, as described by Polonius in *Hamlet*. Once you have read a great book, never let it go – the physical book can leave you, but its essence will remain if you have made it a part of you.

CHAPTER SIX

PUTTING DOWN THE BOOK

*Even when you are not reading, be mindful
of the reading that you have done and have yet to do.
Reading is something that we do at many different
times of the day, frequently without awareness. In some
cases, we are reading purely for information — such as
with street signs — but with the reading of fiction,
poetry and other literature, we benefit from mulling
over it, even when it is not in front of us. Embracing
your reading even when you are not actually
doing it is a part of reading mindfully.*

Keeping the Book in Mind

For the avid reader, it can be a habit to devour a book, staying up all night to finish it, neglecting friends, children and work to read it, and then — to forget it. For some, the moment they put down the book, it is gone from their minds, and may be permanently deleted. For the mindful reader, this is a habit to overcome, as all good books should become a part of us forever.

OF COURSE, SOME BOOKS are more important to take to heart than others — a thriller may not be something that you want to reflect on too much, whereas an informative non-fiction read or a work of classic literature will be something you would like to remember. But even a thriller is worth reflecting on for a period, making the odd note about and scanning for a brilliant quote. Every writer puts a huge amount of effort, time and thought into their books, even the page-turners that are light and addictive.

Each book you read should have some memorable moments, quotes and ideas. With a crime novel or thriller, there may be scenes you would rather forget, but there may also be moments of wonder, emotional understanding and intelligence that are worth mulling over. With a fluffy romance, the same could be true — you as a reader can ask yourself what it was you loved about the book, and whether you want to take any of its lessons into your own romantic

MINDFULNESS EXERCISE

FINISHING MINDFULLY

✳

When you put down the book you have just finished, do so mindfully. First put it on your lap and think about it. What did you learn from it? Did you learn facts, or was your emotional intelligence expanded? Did you enjoy the narrative voice, the tone of the writer and their writing style? What can you compare it to? Are there other books you have read that are similar? If there are, note them down in your reading journal. Or perhaps there are books you read as a child that this book reminds you of? Pick up your reading notebook and write in it. Write down any book it makes you think of; you can then look at it again to remind yourself about it in more depth. Would you recommend this book to others? Write down their names. Are there particular passages you loved? Make sure they are marked. Was there anything about it you hated? Think about why you didn't like those passages, and what they made you feel or think about. Would you like to read more by this author? Spend some time researching them.

Now decide where you are going to put the book. Are you going to lend it to someone? Keep it for future reference? Take it to a charity shop? Or leave it in a public place for someone to pick up? If you are going to put it in your home library to keep, put it in the right place. See the following pages for more advice on this.

life. When it comes to more serious literature, there may be passages that you would like to highlight and return to, to study and even memorize. And with informative literature, you will probably want to go back and remember the parts that seemed most important and interesting to you.

DE-CLUTTER YOUR LIBRARY

◆

Every six months, or at least once every year, it is a good idea to address the state of your library. Whether you live in a large house with many floors where you can keep hundreds of books, or in a tiny flat where space is at a premium and every book should be carefully selected, it is worthwhile periodically attacking your library and mindfully de-cluttering it of unnecessary books.

Alphabeticize

The best way to do this is to arrange all of your books in alphabetical order, either by title or author's name. If you prefer, it can be a good idea to have two sections – fiction and non-fiction, each of them alphabeticized. Start at the letter A, and work through your book collection. Take each book off the shelf, dust it and hold it in your hands for a moment. Feel its weight, touch its cover, run your finger over the title. Open the book at a random spot, and glance at a few lines. Remember what it was about. Allow yourself to drift into that world for a moment or two.

Keep or Pass On

Now decide whether you want to keep it. Will you ever read it again? Does it mean something to you? Would you enjoy giving it to someone? Who would that person be? Might they gain something from this book? Would giving them the book act as a kind of message from you, or would it simply be a gesture of joy in the love of reading?

If you decide to give it to someone you know would appreciate it, put it in a pile with the person's name on a bookmark. If you realize you will never re-read this book, and it would be better off going on to live another life, put it in a pile for donating to a charity shop.

Consider also, if it is a book you really loved reading and would like to share with the rest of the world, leaving it in a public place for someone to find – for instance, a park bench, a café or a train station. Write a note on a card and slip it inside the front cover, for the next reader to find. Tell them why you loved the book, in a few words.

Decrease by Ten Per Cent

When de-cluttering your library, you should aim to rehome at least ten per cent of your books. This gives you an opportunity to buy more books – or slim down your excess of volumes. As you work through your collection, enjoy dusting them, caressing them and taking a momentary journey with each one. You will need to do this on a day when nothing else is going on – do it on a weekend, and if you have children, ask them to do the same with their own libraries. Encourage them to work mindfully through their shelves, pondering which books they want to keep forever, which they might give to a friend and which they might give to a charity shop, their local library or school. They will find that they enjoy the process of freeing up space on their shelves, while re-living some of their favourite reads, and you can compare notes at the end of the day. Who has created the biggest pile to pass on? Who discovered treasured books that they had forgotten about? Share these books at the end of the day, delighting in those stories that you loved, perhaps reading some to each other before they go back on the shelf, or get passed on to a favourite cousin, friend or younger relative.

Curating Your Collection

For an even more rigorous library overhaul, those who enjoy the process of curating and listing can create an index of their library. How many of us lend out our books, then never get them back? Buy yourself an embosser or a collection of stickers for the front of your books. These will mark that this book is 'From the library of . . . read and return!'. This will add to your sense of owning the book and help you decide what to do with it– do you want to keep it enough to put your mark on it forever? If you don't, that is a good sign that you ought to give that book away.

Use a card index to write down every book you own. Use one card per book. Write on the card the title of the book, author's name, date purchased and date read. Then, whenever you get a new book, you can add a card to the library collection and file it. If you lend the book to someone, write on the card who you have lent it to. For some, this could be taking library curation too far – you might prefer to let your books flow in and out of your life in a less controlled way. Whatever your preference, the dusting and cleansing of the library is in itself a mindful process that will give you a great deal of meaningful reflection and pleasure.

Consider the Characters in Your Books

Be mindful of your reading, even when you are not reading. Think of the characters in books that you have most admired. Periodically, walk along the books in your library, allowing one hand to touch every spine. Let the titles drift past you – do this in a state of flow. This means that you are avoiding thinking about this activity consciously, and instead letting titles sing out to you. If a title does claim your attention, let your hand stop there. Touch the book. Take it off the shelf and flick through it. Remember the characters in the book. Is there one that stands out? Is something they did of moral and emotional interest? For instance, if the book that your hand lands on is *Zorba the Greek* by Nikos Kazantzakis, then you will think about how Zorba dealt with his everyday difficulties by dancing. Whenever he was in a difficult situation, he danced. He danced away his worries, his anger and his pain, and he found his answers in dance. Think about this for a minute. Could you do the same? Then carry on through your bookshelves. You may stumble across Joseph Conrad's *Heart of Darkness*. In this book, Charles Marlow travelled deep into the innermost corners of his own heart, and found chaos and death. His behaviour may cause you to ponder how you would cope in such a situation. You might come to *The Great Gatsby*, and think of the vanity and tragedy of this man's life. As your fingers move along your shelves, each book will speak to you about another human you have learnt from, whether fictional or real.

The lives you have lived through reading these books all feed into your knowledge of the world and of yourself.

Each time you go back to your library to do this exercise, you will remember different characters in your books and how they react to life in different parts of history, different parts of the world and different cultures. The lives you have lived through reading these books all feed into your knowledge of the world and of yourself. If you mindfully engage in exercise regularly, you will benefit repeatedly from your own library, and the exercise will also help you to keep abreast of which books you should keep and which you should pass on.

MINDFULNESS EXERCISE

CREATE FOOD DESCRIBED IN A BOOK

✳

One of the loveliest ways to appreciate a book after finishing reading it is to cook some of the foods that are described in its pages. Create food that is described in the book, for example, the omelette in *The Debt to Pleasure* by John Lanchester, or the garlic snails in *Babette's Feast* by Karen Blixen, or the Italian pasta dishes in *The Food of Love* by Anthony Capella. Cook these and eat them while re-reading the relevant extract from the book. Be inspired by the foods in books that you read, and try to re-create their dishes, whether it is the slab of bread with bacon that Joe Gargery gives to Pip in *Great Expectations*, or the emotionally powerful soups and desserts created in Laura Esquivel's *Like Water for Chocolate*. This is another great way to 'put down the book' but still be mindful of its message and its purpose. Make the madeleines from *Remembrance of Things Past* by Marcel Proust, and meditate upon the memories that come into your mind as you eat the madeleine. Does it conjure up memories from your own childhood, or does it simply remind you of reading the passage in Proust? Whichever it does, savour the moment to the full – breathe in the aroma, savour the delicious flavours and enjoy whatever memories it brings. In this way, life is rejoined after reading the book, and your reading has brought greater appreciation of life both past and present. This is why putting down the book, and then mindfully bringing the book into your real life is so valuable.

MINDFULNESS EXERCISE

MULLING IT OVER

❋

Next time you finish a book, allow yourself ten minutes to think about it mindfully. Think about how you would describe this book to a friend. What are the main points you feel it would be worth passing on? If it was non-fiction, what did you learn from it that was most memorable and significant? Think about what you would like to add to the book yourself. Could you expand on it? What questions would you ask the author? If it was fiction, cogitate the drama of the novel or short story. What did you feel about it? How did it relate to your life? Do you think the author achieved what they set out to do? Would you add an extra chapter, and if so, what would happen in it? Think about the idea that often what is not said in a book is what is most important. Was there anything implied in the book that you have just read, which was not spelt out, and which you are now thinking about? Are there some enigmas unsolved which the author deliberately left for you to work out for yourself?

Take a moment to jot down:
- three major points of the book
- three questions you would ask the author
- three ways it relates to you
- three ways it relates to people you know

Tell the next person you meet about the book, whoever they are – a shop-keeper, a railway passenger next to you, your mother or a telemarketing salesman who is trying to sell you solar panels. Putting your thoughts into words will help to distil your feelings about the book. Persuade them to read it if they haven't already, which will in turn make you consider what you admired about the book yourself. If they have read it, all the better, as you can enter into a debate about its qualities. Don't stop here – find someone else to discuss the book with, who may have a profoundly different opinion.

Conclusion

There are many ways to enhance your life by reading mindfully. These methods will help you to read more meaningfully, bringing your life to books and books into your life equally. We have discussed how you can choose your books more carefully, and keep your library mindfully streamlined. Rather than buying books online, go into a bookshop. Read books in public and strike up conversations. Enjoy giving books away. Relish every word. Ponder each sentence, read aloud whenever possible, and share your reading. Or take the opposite extreme of an approach, and dive in and let the words wash over you – both methods are valid to the mindful reader, as described in Chapter One.

Now is the time to put down this book, and contemplate what you have learnt. Write down some thoughts in your reading journal. If you are pressed for time, write a six-word memoir of this book; then re-read the book and allow yourself to enjoy it completely and mindfully.

'Beware the man of one book,
as he will have only one perspective on life.'
ST THOMAS AQUINAS (1225–1274)

FURTHER READING

◆

Non-fiction

The End of Your Life Book Club by Will Schwalbe (Two Roads, 2012)

At Home with Books: How Booklovers Live with and Care for Their Libraries by Estelle Ellis and Caroline Seebohm (Thames & Hudson, 2006)

Howards End is on the Landing: A Year of Reading from Home by Susan Hill (Profile Books, 2010)

How Proust can Change Your Life by Alain de Botton (Picador, 2006)

How to Read a Book: The Classic Guide to Intelligent Reading by Mortimer J. Adler and Charles Van Doren (Touchstone, 2008)

Leave me Alone, I'm Reading: Finding and Losing Myself in Books by Maureen Corrigan (Vintage Books, 2007)

Mindfulness: How to Live Well by Paying Attention by Ed Halliwell (Hay House, 2015)

The Year of Reading Dangerously: How Fifty Great Books Saved My Life by Andy Miller (Fourth Estate, 2015)

The Novel Cure: An A–Z of Literary Remedies by Ella Berthoud and Susan Elderkin (Canongate, 2013)

Out of Sheer Rage: In the Shadow of D. H. Lawrence by Geoff Dyer (Canongate, 2015)

Packing my Library: An Elegy and Ten Digressions by Alberto Manguel (Yale University Press, 2018)

A Passion for Books by Harold Rabinowitz and Rob Kaplan (Times Books, 2001)

The Possessed: Adventures with Russian Books and the People Who Read Them by Elif Batuman (Granta Books, 2018)

A Reader on Reading by Alberto Manguel (Yale University Press, 2011)

Reading Lolita in Tehran by Azar Nafisi (Penguin, 2015)

The Rights of the Reader by Daniel Pennac (Walker Books, 2006)

Ruined by Reading: A Life in Books by Lynn Sharon Schwartz (Beacon Press, 1997)

The Story Cure: An A–Z of Books to Keep Kids Happy, Healthy and Wise by Ella Berthoud and Susan Elderkin (Canongate, 2016)

Fiction

Fahrenheit 451 by Ray Bradbury
(Flamingo Modern Classics, 1999)

If on a Winter's Night a Traveller by Italo
Calvino (Vintage Classics, 2007)

The Uncommon Reader by Alan Bennett
(Faber & Faber, 2008)

84 Charing Cross Road by Helene Hanff
(Sphere, 1982)

The Bookshop by Penelope Fitzgerald
(Fourth Estate, 2018)

The Bookshop on the Corner by Jenny
Colgan (William Morrow Paperbacks,
2016)

The Haunted Bookshop by Christopher
Morley (1st World Library, 2007)

The Jane Austen Book Club by Karen Joy
Fowler (Penguin, 2005)

The Little Paris Bookshop Nina George
(Abacus, 2015)

Mr Penumbra's 24-Hour Bookstore by
Robin Sloan (Atlantic Books, 2014)

The Neverending Story by Michael Ende
(Puffin, 2014)

The Paper House by Carlos Maria
Dominguez (Harvill Secker, 2005)

The Readers of Broken Wheel Recommend
by Katarina Bivald (Vintage, 2016)

Titles mentioned in the book

An Evil Cradling by Brian Keenan
(Vintage, 1993)

Basho: The Complete Haiku by Matsuo
Bashō (Kodansha America, 2013)

*Not Quite What I was Planning: Six Word
Memoirs by Writers Famous and Obscure* by
Larry Smith (HarperCollins, 2008)

Tess of the D'Urbervilles by Thomas
Hardy (Penguin Classics, 2003)

Websites

Be Mindful
bemindful.co.uk/

Mindfulness Association
www.mindfulnessassociation.net/

The School of Life's videos on
literature
www.youtube.com/
watch?v=4RCFLobfqcw

INDEX

ACKNOWLEDGEMENTS

◆

I would like to thank my three brothers and my father for providing
me with the best reading nook ever – in the form of a swinging chair – in
which I have written much of this book. It looks just like the one on the cover. I
could not have written any of this volume without having first written *The Novel Cure*
and *The Story Cure* with Susan Elderkin, with whom many of these ideas were first
thrashed through. I would also like to thank Ashish Ranpura for his help with thinking
about mindfulness in a scientific way. And my husband Carl for reading aloud with
such élan on a daily basis, and my three children for being willing participants in
their own adventures in mindful reading. A huge thank you to Monica Perdoni
for starting the whole thing off, and to Kate Shanahan for being an artistic
catalyst. Thanks also to my editor Caroline Earle, as well as
Jane Roe for her careful copy-editing.

Most importantly, thanks to all the reading mentors in my life
who gave me books that I could lose and find myself in at all stages of life –
to my father for the campfire reading, to my mother for her omnivorous approach to
books, to my teachers Mrs Day at Queenswood School for encouraging ferocious
reading and Mark Moore at Marlborough College for his passionate approach, as well
as David Holbrook at Downing College, Cambridge for helping us to take it all apart
And thanks to all the readers who still love the feel of a book in their hands.